DEDICATION

F

In your memory I continue.

N

Home Rules

Principal photography by

Fernando Bengoechea
John Bessler
François Dischinger

Nate Berkus
with Barri Leiner

Home Rules
Transform the Place You Live
into a Place You'll Love

HYPERION

Copyright © 2005
Nate Berkus Entertainment, Inc.
Photographs © 2005
Fernando Bengoechea and John Bessler and
Jonn Coolidge and François Dischinger
and Andrew Eccles, and Tim Street-Porter

All rights reserved.
No part of this book may be used or
reproduced in any manner whatsoever
without the written permission of the Publisher.
Printed in the United States of America.

For information address:
Hyperion
77 West 66th Street
New York, New York 10023-6298

ISBN 1-4013-0137-1

Hyperion books are available
for special promotions and premiums.
For details contact Michael Rentas,
Assistant Director, Inventory Operations,
Hyperion,
77 West 66th Street, 11th floor,
New York, New York 10023,
or call 212-456-0133.

Produced by
SMALLWOOD & STEWART, INC.
5 East 20th Street
New York, New York 10003
Designed by Lisa Yee

First Edition
10 9 8 7 6 5 4 3 2 1

contents

introduction

"making your home your greatest pleasure is a luxury we all need to indulge"

There's no greater pleasure than to love the way you live. A home should be a reflection of your lifestyle and tell the story of the people who reside there over the years. As our lives evolve, so should our interiors. Like getting a new haircut, waking up your wardrobe, or working up to a new workout routine, redecorating is about making a change. Even the smallest update or organization idea can result in R&R (renewal and rejuvenation). It should be your pleasure to walk through the front door each evening—home to a house filled with meaning and memories. The idea of living well has always been important to me. It's the best investment you can make in your well-being. Oprah always says your home is the place to invest your money and energy. Your home is where you live, not just physically but spiritually and emotionally as well.

While I haven't had formal training in the field, my passion for travel, exploring cultural arts, and furniture design—along with an interior-decorating mom—has made design an integral part of my life. In September 2002, I found myself in the very bright spotlight of *The Oprah Winfrey Show.* Oprah gave me the opportunity to share my decorating ideas with you and show how they could improve the way you live. Through my work on television and a few makeovers later, I began to see how my ideas and enthusiasm made people want to make changes both small and large—the kind that made them feel better about their homes and themselves.

I'm overwhelmed and moved by the thousands of letters filled with your stories and the inspiration you found after one of my decorating experiments caught your eye. I'm able to connect on a personal level with my firm's clients, so I wondered how I could better connect with you, the viewers and audience members out there, who I may never have the chance to meet. (Who knows, maybe your makeover moment is next?) Your inquiries and interest made me want to answer all of your questions and help decorate all of your homes. You made me want to give back. I hope you will consider this book the biggest thank you note I've ever written.

I started to think about what I have to share with you and realized I actually live by a fairly firm set of design ideals. With practice, experience, and a few mistakes, I've developed guidelines that I call *Home Rules.* This isn't math; there's no right answer for every space but rather a mix of what I've learned works best. At the end of the day a room should be a beautiful reflection of who you are and what you love. I'll just give you a frame to work within, for every decorating challenge and room in the house.

Think of this book as an appointment with me. Let's experiment together, hit the flea market, head to the paint store, and even clean house with some organization revelations. Each chapter will help you decide the way you want your home to look and feel, one room at a time. I'll teach you how to ask yourself the important questions that get a project started and how to take the first steps. We'll go behind the scenes to some of my favorite makeovers (wish there was room for all of them) and share before-and-after secrets, sources, and shops. I'll even take you home with me. Along the way I'll give you design ideas and talk about how to twist a few of the rules to make them your own.

Take in your surroundings, respect where you've been, and get excited about where we can go. Remember, it's your home, and you have to decide what you can live with, live without, and really love having around. So put the coffee on—I'm coming over for a visit. I hope you'll be at home.

Live well,

nb

1

Getting Started

Inspirations

Everyone can learn to decorate, on any budget. The trick is to define the colors you love, styles of furniture that move you, and be open to change and inspiration. Be willing to take a few risks along the way—that is how I've created my favorite interiors. Why not buy that antique lamp you love and figure out where it goes later?

Decorating or redecorating your home isn't something you have to take on all at once or with a big bank balance. The most important first steps are deciding which changes will make the most impact and bring you the most pleasure and which can wait. Grab a notebook so you can collect your design ideas and jot down your decorating dreams. Try to divide them into projects that you can accomplish in a day or a week or a month and those

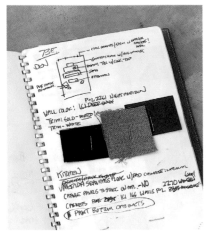

that will take a long-term commitment.

Look for inspiration anywhere and everywhere. Rent a movie or head to the theater in search of beautiful or interesting stage sets. A trip to the museum can make you feel as if you've stepped into the future or back in time; an exhibit of Japanese glazed pottery can spark a new display idea for the mantel; even the curator's choice of paint color can inspire. Visit your local historical society for a look at your town's past, or attend house and garden tours that let you past the garden gate and into your neighbors' homes. You'd be amazed at what you can bring home from a sneak peek. Emulating what works well, and making those ideas your own, is an art in itself.

There are also places to go for inspiration that aren't quite so literal, the emotional and literary "light bulbs" in your life: How does a passage in a book make you feel? Keep your notebook by your bedside and write down end-of-the-day thoughts, wishes, and feelings. Close your eyes and imagine your "dream" space. What do you see? This soulful approach can inspire your best and most focused thinking about achieving the room you long for.

"where do you start?
in the room where you'd like
to live your best"

ten questions to ask yourself
what's your style?

WELL NOTED | I always keep a wish list of ideas in the back of my design notebook (opposite); it's an ever-changing inventory of things that inspire me.

1 What kind of surroundings make you happy? A simple and airy space that feels like the beach, or a cozy room filled with books and a comfortable chair?

2 Do you respond to neat and organized or chock-full of accessories?

3 Which is your favorite room in the house? Which is your least favorite?

4 Where do you feel most at home? Are you city sleek or country casual?

5 How much time, energy, and money are you willing to spend right now? Next month? In a year?

6 If you could change one thing about your home today, what would it be?

7 Do you have a favorite piece of furniture or art or collectible object that could be a starting point?

8 Where would you take a dream vacation? Could you translate that feeling to your home?

9 Which people inspire you? How do they live?

10 Do your decorating dreams correspond to the way you actually live? Does a formal living room really fit in with your casual entertaining?

interior motives: creating a style file

A TRIP TO INSPIRATION

Movies can be an endless source of inspiration for your decorating projects. Here are a few of my all-time personal favorite design-inspiring films:

Auntie Mame
Casino
The Fountainhead
Howards End
Interiors
The Philadelphia Story
Pillow Talk
Sabrina
Something's Gotta Give

Design ideas can be found almost anywhere. A cup of rich dark espresso can spark a color scheme for your bedroom, while a family room featured in a design book might inspire a moment of makeover magic of your own.

Leaf through home magazines and catalogs; carry a digital camera and take snapshots of rooms, colors, fabric, and furniture you like. Don't think too long; follow your gut reactions. I tape bits of fabrics and paint swatches I'm considering into my design notebook. I also write down furniture measurements and the addresses of design resources I find along the way.

Focus your thoughts. I always ask clients to make their own style file and to bring it to our first consultation. We talk about how they want to feel in their house (calm? sophisticated? casual? sexy?). Sometimes people are able to express what they don't like more easily than what they do: "I dislike dark spaces"; "Too much furniture makes me feel claustrophobic"; "I'm not a fan of floral fabric." This kind of input helps me develop an idea of their decorating vision and expectations.

Look at your likes and dislikes. Begin to sort your ideas into rooms and priorities. Figure out the amount of time you'd like to give to your project, and look at your budget.

"waking at dawn and waiting for the gates to open—flea market finds are heaven"

shop talk

One of the most exciting changes in home decorating has been the explosion of good design options at the mass-market level. In the same way that high fashion seems to race off the runways and into the local mall, less expensive interpretations of furniture and decorative accessories are showing up and showing off their good looks in mainstream retailers faster than you can say "television makeover." These establishments, as well as their catalog counterparts, are the best places to look for upholstered sofas, chairs, throws, and pillows at a fair price. Vases, lamps, bed linens, towels, and ready-made curtains are typically in stock and ready to ship or take home.

The Internet. Even small local antiques shops have websites today, so you don't have to travel beyond your desktop for special pieces. To get the most useful results, be as specific as possible in your search. If you see something you like, don't be shy about asking the dealer a lot of questions. Check the dimensions and condition of the item and ask about any wear. Double-check the price, as well as shipping costs and delivery time; it may not be a good buy if shipping and handling nearly doubles the price or delivery takes longer than you expected. Confirm your right to return something if there's a problem. Finally, save all your correspondence with the dealer and print out a copy for your files.

Flea markets and swap meets. These are my absolute favorite stomping grounds for accessories, small furnishings with one-of-a-kind style, and interesting objects that have a history. Go online or search your local library and newspaper listings for the best markets or fairgrounds around your area.

PLAN IN HAND

Create a floor plan on a sheet of paper before you make any big purchases. If finding your new furniture lineup (or rearranging your old) is hard to visualize on paper, use blue painter's tape to outline the shape of the furniture on the wall or floor. This special tape leaves no marks when it's removed. Or cut out a template of the piece from a roll of kraft paper.

Whichever method you use, try on an "outline design" and live with it for a while, then walk around it and see how it works for you before you make a move or a purchase.

FROM GOOD TO GREAT

A room or setting where items from completely different price ranges mingle and meet is, for me, a sign of good design.

Picture a modern living room: sleek stone floors, a crisp white sofa, shiny painted tables. Now picture it with a pair of old carved candlesticks from a consignment shop and a well-worn chair covered in new fabric. The room looked good without the old pieces, but with them it gains depth and contrast.

I'm also a huge fan of making over bargain finds—transforming a store-bought bookcase with a rich shade of paint to create a "custom" piece, or dressing up flea market lamps with expensive shades.

FLEA WITH ME | Loose and "lost" pages, prints from old books, or maps from an old atlas are frame-worthy flea market finds. I like collecting in pairs— a couple of chairs and a set of brass candlesticks make the pile; cold old furniture is just waiting for a coat of paint; architectural accents add an instant touch of inherited heritage (opposite).

The earlier you get to a flea market, the better, so wake up with the birds, coffee up, and set out with the following: a tape measure, your design notebook (complete with room measurements and fabric and paint samples), a digital camera, a flashlight, and a friend with great decorating taste. Don't worry about the "book" value of an item; if green pottery speaks to you, and the price is what you're willing to pay, it's the "right" price. And don't be afraid to bargain ("Is this your best price?" "Can you do any better?")—dealers expect it.

Auctions. A live auction is a wonderful place to buy anything from an extra set of dishes to a painting. Unlike the Internet, you can actually handle and examine items and you'll get a far truer sense of color, size, and condition than you would from any photo. Even better, if no one else is interested in the same thing you are on that day, you can pick up some great bargains. It's pretty easy to get caught up in auction fever and wind up paying much more than you planned, so decide on your bidding limit at the outset and once you've reached it, stop.

Thrift, resale, and consignment shops. Whenever I travel, I break open the Yellow Pages to locate these kinds of stores. Resale and consignment shops tend to be a bit more discriminating and selective in their offerings than thrift stores; some even specialize in a "look" and often carry estate pieces. Look for monogrammed flatware and silver frames, a great set of dining chairs, or a wonderful gilt mirror.

bringing nature indoors

NATURALLY SPEAKING

They may not be technically what most of us think of as "nature" when we talk about decorating, but organic materials such as natural fibers, wood floors, twig blinds, or a sea-grass rug are timeless choices for any room. A paint palette inspired by the sand and sea is instantly at home in almost any interior. Bring in the light by painting the ceiling a beautiful shade of pale blue—it will subtly lift the room and everyone's spirits.

Leather adds instant patina to surroundings. It looks best when it's mixed with other textural fibers or with metal. Live with it just as you do with other fabrics; as it wears over time, it only gets better. Even a pair of worn leather cowboy boots or a stack of old leather-bound books displayed on a shelf works well as an accessory to add age and natural interest.

Bringing the outdoors into an interior is one of the easiest and most affordable ways to accessorize. Believe me, Mother Nature really knows how to work a room. The quality of her brand-free offerings creates a simple and effective impression in any decorating style or color scheme. And the idea that you can be transported by a humble detail like a piece of sea glass or a basket of pinecones is simply remarkable.

Collect natural memories. Whenever I go on vacation, I always bring back a small rock or a shell that has caught my eye as a tangible reminder of my travels. A piece of driftwood becomes a centerpiece on the dining room table. Seashells slip between stacks on the bookshelves.

Make good use of greens. Hit the backyard for unusual leaves and greenery; placed in a simple vase or glass, they have a sculptural quality. Keep a green leaf in a small glass bottle on the kitchen sink; place a pair of tailored ivy or herb topiaries in natural clay pots on your mantel.

Enjoy fresh flowers every day. Roses trimmed short and tight in a silver cup or a few wildflowers in a humble juice glass are always beautiful, especially if the arrangement is kept simple. Put a single stem in a vase on the windowsill, the powder-room sink, or a night table for a splash of color. A bunch of hydrangea in a galvanized pail or an ice bucket is more inviting than a studied bouquet.

DOWN TO EARTH | (Clockwise from top left): An elegant black-and-white photograph as a window to the great outdoors; coral fragments and sea fans from the shore; sand-filled glass hurricane lamps; a tight bouquet of peonies in a mercury glass cup; a single tropical leaf in a clear glass vase; sea glass and shells and African beads; dried magnolia pods and vintage coral beads; and a driftwood lamp.

luxe for less

MIXING OLD AND NEW | An art student's model, a vintage box, and a small bouquet of cream and pink roses make an interesting vignette (opposite). Treating yourself to the "extras" when you're the only company coming to dinner will make it feel good to walk through the front door every day.

You can make your home special without spending a fortune. Here are some ideas that offer big impact.

Small luxuries, big dividends. Good sheets, plush towels, down pillows, and fine soaps make you feel pampered. Splurge on the highest quality you can afford, one special purchase at a time. Build up to the bigger items gradually.

Enjoy candlelight and fresh flowers. Scented candles and small votives should be considered an everyday treat along with a once-a-week flower purchase, even if it's just a single stem from the grocery store. If fresh flowers are unavailable, consider branches of berries or bowls of fresh apples, lemons, or pomegranates.

Add dressmaker details. Dress up pillows, curtains, and lampshades with ribbon trim. With just a few yards of a favorite fabric you can have a custom-made throw or beautiful pillows.

Get framed. Art exists on every level and will always enhance your home. From cherished items such as a child's artwork or a family photograph in a handsome frame to engravings taken from an art book or a pressed fern picked from the garden, surround yourself with beautiful things on your walls.

Create "architecture." Consider custom details or salvage finds such as crown moldings, mantels, built-in bookcases, heavy doors, or fine hardware to make a room feel grand.

"pairing items from completely different price ranges is a sign of good design"

"antiques stores always seem to be
waving me right in off the road"

home rules
discover your look

ANTIQUES TALK | Visit antiques and collectibles shops for one-of-a-kind finishings and furnishings (opposite). Sometimes a credit card or a small refundable deposit can afford you the opportunity to see how a serendipitous discovery will look, feel, and fit in before you make it your own.

1 A big budget isn't always a necessity. Small luxuries can have more impact than big-ticket items.

2 Don't be afraid to experiment. Making mistakes is often the only way to discover what you like.

3 One authentic piece is better than a house full of reproductions.

4 A single style statement should never be used top to toe. Mixing high and low, old and new, keeps things interesting.

5 Keep careful records of all pertinent information in a notebook—style numbers, measurements, paint colors, inspirations.

6 Get in on auction action. I've discovered some of my best makeover magic at auctions, both live and online.

7 Make friends with your tape measure: Ready-to-go options such as window treatments can save you money.

8 Diversify your shopping—department stores, online, catalogs, and flea markets—to take advantage of the best each has to offer.

9 Buy a piece you love. Eventually it will make its way into your decor.

10 Look everywhere for inspiration, then add to your own personal vision.

2

At Home with
Color

Color is the decorating glue that holds your home together. A beautiful scheme—even if it's simply different shades of white—can make your whole house seem thoughtful, well-planned, and organized.

Even though color plays such an important role in the way our homes look and how we feel about them, there are no hard-and-fast rules about finding the right palette. Color choices are personal; start with what you love. In the end, what works for you is the right decision. Deciding on a scheme doesn't have to be overwhelming. There are reliable ways to find the colors that please you.

Explore your emotional "color quotient": What moves you? What makes you happy? Or calm? Or energized? A treasured object, the lipstick your mother wore, a painting you've always admired—just about anything can serve

as inspiration. I'm crazy about camel; it reminds me of a sport coat I had as a kid. Adults always seemed to include me in their conversations when I wore it, so today that color makes me feel grown up and comfortable. Maybe the starting point for you is the view through your window, a piece of furniture in the room, a fabric you've always wanted to use.

Another great place to explore your inner color wheel is your clothes closet—it tells you what colors you like to be around day after day.

Paint, the quickest way to bring color into your home, is inexpensive and simple to change, so you can experiment until you're satisfied. Other ways of introducing color—fabric, wallpaper, rugs—are a little more permanent, so I prefer to stick with more neutral tones. I'm partial to solid grays, whites, and beiges for the big items that can't easily be changed, saving patterns and brights for quick picks like towels, pillows, pottery, or even decorative trim.

So take this guided tour for a full-color picture of how to craft a palette you will love to live with.

"color cues can come from just about anywhere"

ten questions to ask yourself
which hue is you?

CLOTHES CALL | Borrow clues, cues, and hues from your wardrobe (opposite). The familiarity of these everyday shades can translate easily into a relaxed and meaningful color scheme for a room. Spend a few minutes in the paint shop matching up color chips with your favorite outfits—this idea is sure to jump-start a pleasing palette.

1 What's your favorite color? Open a box of crayons and pick the first color that catches your eye.

2 How do you react to color? Do the warm shades of a sunset move you? Or is it the clean, clear coolness of a winter landscape that speaks to you?

3 What's in your clothes closet? Does that one red sweater get passed over time and time again for the neutrals in your wardrobe?

4 How big is the space? Do you want it to feel larger or cozier?

5 If you're decorating more than one room, do you want to unify them with color?

6 How do you want to feel in the room—laid-back and relaxed or excited and energized?

7 What's the room's current scheme? Are you already living with colors you like, or are you looking for a change?

8 How much available light is there? What time of day will you use the room most?

9 Is there a color memory you want to call up? A place you want to re-create? A mood you want to capture?

10 Are you decorating a room with a view? Do you want to incorporate the hues in your surroundings into the palette?

"call out color in your choices
of details and accessories"

tap the power of color

Color not only affects mood, but can also play with perspective and the scale of a room. Here are a few tips and tricks that can rework the way a room looks and feels.

Make a small space seem larger. Use soft, cool hues like pale gray, ivory, or light blue, with white or ivory accents. Paint ceilings and ceiling molding white to draw the eye upward.

Make a large space seem smaller. A cavernous space is a great place to use deep, rich colors; they bring the walls a little closer. Paint the trim or ceiling in the same color for a luminous effect.

Play up small spaces. Dark, warm colors can make them seem more intimate and important. Try chocolate brown, navy blue, or deep green. Or raise their temperature—and their status—with a bright color on the walls or an energetic wallpaper.

Go room to room. If you're painting two or more spaces that open from one to another, use the same color or a slightly lighter or darker shade of the same color. Otherwise, the overall area may look disconnected.

Add special effects. Highlight wide or architecturally distinctive trim with a shade of white. A slightly grayed white can give new moldings the patina of age and authenticity. (Paint undistinguished trim the same color as the walls for a uniform effect.)

Lighten up. No color decision has to be forever, so go ahead and try that fun fabric on a side chair or that outrageous orange on your wall.

HUES FLASH

• Paint the inside of bookcases or glass-front cabinets in a contrasting shade.

• Refresh the trim in your bedroom with a fresh coat of white paint.

• Change your accent colors with the seasons: Those warm and wintry plaid pillows and that dark green throw can give way to cool and sleek linen pillows and a bright throw in summer.

• Give a vintage piece of furniture a modern makeover with a bright-colored coat of paint.

COLOR CONFIDENCE | Balance intense color with neutrals (opposite). The sophisticated silvery gray of the velvet club chairs and a steely lamp base set off the acid-green wall and the accessories.

four is a magic number

When you plan your color scheme, **think of creating a layered palette of shades and textures.** Begin with one central color (usually the wall color, but it could be the sofa fabric, the window treatments, or the rug), then introduce three more colors: for example, the walls (color number 1), molding and trim (number 2), a fabric on the sofa (number 3), and accent pillows (number 4). Using four compatible colors should add up to a sophisticated room. On these pages are eight of my favorite combinations. Give them a try—four's a charm.

EIGHT GREAT PALETTES

classic
Cream, camel, white, and black

Nice in natural knits and glazed linens. The combination feels very Roman—timeless yet enduring and sound. It's easy to move accent colors in and out of this framework and to play up textures.

modern
Olive green, pale gray-blue, khaki, and rust

A contemporary combination of muted shades and tones, best achieved through patternless, textural solids like glazed linens and wools.

garden
Pale pink, charcoal, parchment, and silver

Dinner and dancing: Sheer satins and light-weight wools float like evening wear, and shimmering bits of silver feel like perpetual candlelight. Soft and understated. The perfect complement to gently curved lines.

beach
**Nantucket blue, white, and sand,
with a sail of orange**

Sport this updated nautical palette in a den, boy's room, or bath. Experiment with technical nylons, crisp cottons, and striping. Perfect mates.

preppy
Khaki, kelly green, pale blue, and clean white

A crisp white cotton slipcover meets a splash of kelly green paint on the walls. Ice blue pillows in a shimmery finish match the backs of bookcases. A pair of khaki chairs with white piping keep the whole look grounded in its country-club roots.

EIGHT GREAT PALETTES

sexy
Lilac, white, gray, and brown

Lilac silk curtains sweep against gray walls, white trim, and warm brown accents in pillows, throws, or a velvety sofa. A sophisticated combination for a bedroom or living room, surprisingly romantic.

pop
Hot pink, orange, white, and linen

A palette with personality and punch. Vibrant pink and orange bedding against creamy walls with white trim is grounded by a natural sisal carpet and a linen-covered chair or headboard. A foursome that is both brave and bold.

handsome
Navy, royal blue, white, and black

Start with a white sofa or bedding, add a dark blue throw, and accent with patterned pillows in royal blue. White and navy feel retro when combined with black painted furniture, vintage black-and-white tile, or black trim (on a shower curtain, for example). Future forward, but rooted in the past.

let there be bright

An old lighting factory may not seem like the brightest place to bring your bride-to-be, but when it's a spacious loft in a hip Chicago neighborhood, she might be more than a little impressed. Bachelor Dave Hernandez's fiancée, Theresa Surrat, wanted the loft to become more feminine and more like a real home, not just a storage area for Dave's quirky collections.

Like many industrial spaces, this one had super-high ceilings and soaring brick walls, but it was dark as a basement. The solution began with the addition of color and light to give it warmth and personality. Only one tiny "porthole" illuminated the entire loft, so I broke through a brick wall and installed a nine-foot-square paned window. An electric shade ensures that light floods in, but there's still plenty of privacy.

The floors got a splash of glossy orange patio paint, which instantly added energy to the space. Painting the wall behind the living room seating area a deep gray gave it drama and impact.

I felt that the loft's high ceilings and factory feel would be best complemented by furniture with modern lines and simple fabrics. A thick, shaggy rug, known as a flokati, added a sixties vibe. Removing a bookcase opened up a corner, making way for a glass dining table and clear chairs floating on another sexy flokati. To create a gallery-like area for some of Dave's collections, the walls were reframed and the inset display cases lighted and painted orange.

Up the stairs, on a sleeping platform, we knocked out a half wall to open up the space and replaced it with metal railings made from plumbing pipes that continue down the steps. The signature orange color found its way here, too, adding a jolt to a subdued palette of grays and browns and creating a pleasing contrast.

The only thing left to add to this makeover was one happy couple.

THE CHALLENGE Make a bride-to-be feel at home | Define good
spaces for entertaining and dining | Keep it clean and modern
without becoming cold | Create a showplace for collections | Lighten
up the industrial look

"it's easy to have a crush on orange when it's paired with creamy neutrals"

nudes are a bit rude for mixed company

go for striking, not biking

GOOD COUPLES | Pairs of luminous glass lamps and classic Barcelona chairs (left) frame the seating area in the open floor plan. Velvet and sleek finishes like leather, chrome, and glass, along with the mirrored coffee table, are sexy and sophisticated.

TURN ON THE BRIGHTS | Replacing the loft's simple plywood floor would have been too pricey, so it was livened up with warm orange paint, inspired by the finish on Dave's motorcycle, now a piece of movable art in the room (below). The huge window that replaced the tiny original one floods the room with natural light.

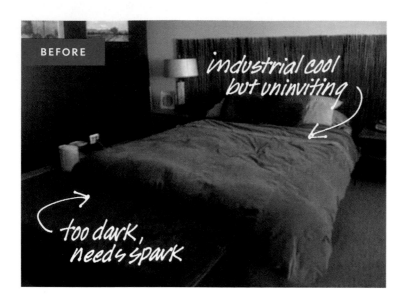

BEFORE

industrial cool but uninviting

too dark, needs spark

SNAP DECISION | An orange color scheme infuses the gray industrial space with vibrancy and life (below). Because the walls lacked architectural detail, I created colored insets to spotlight Dave's collections, here a group of vintage cameras.

RISE TO THE OCCASION | At the touch of a switch, the hydraulic headboard-night table combination rolls up to reveal storage space (opposite). On the bed, bold accents contrast with the more neutral khaki and gray linens.

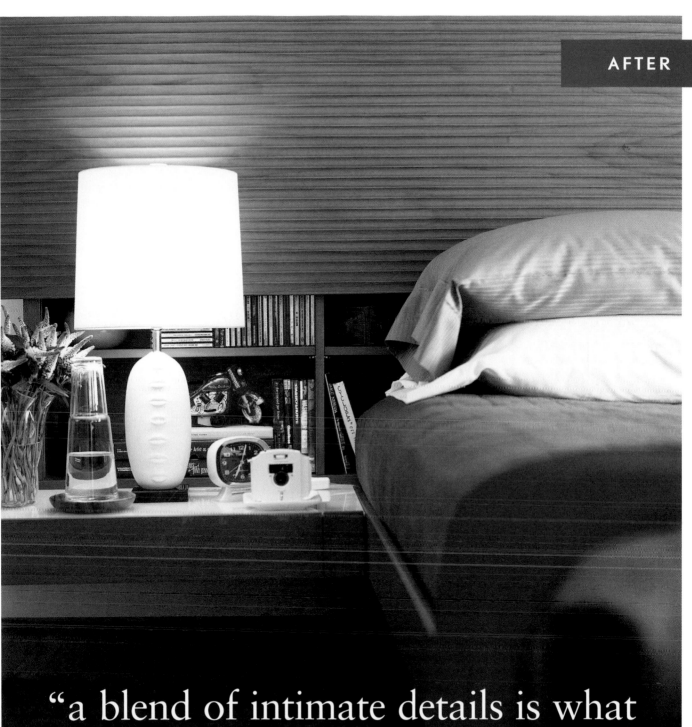

"a blend of intimate details is what makes a place yours"

in the right light

LOOKING GOOD

♦ Put all your lights on dimmers, even those in the bathroom. This will allow you to alter the mood of the room instantly.

♦ Warm up a bathroom by using a mix of mood lighting and brighter task lighting.

♦ Use lower-wattage bulbs to create a more intimate effect in a room.

♦ A pair of table lamps will cast a more pleasing light than a single bright source.

♦ Paint the inside of a nonfabric lampshade the palest pink— it will make everyone look a little younger.

Good lighting enhances any room. It provides instant mood and atmosphere, and changes the way we see our rooms and ourselves—low light makes dark, rich colors and rooms even more intimate, and bright light makes a vibrant color appear more intense.

Use multiple sources. One light fixture in a room can't serve all your needs. An overhead light provides general illumination, but it should be supplemented by task lighting for working or reading, while for dining or simply brightening a dark corner you may prefer softer light.

Overhead lighting. Except for chandeliers, when the fixture itself makes a design statement, I like to keep overhead lighting to a minimum. It's a necessity in kitchens and bathrooms, where I recommend recessed fixtures, which can be directed where they're most needed.

Task lighting. Kitchens, bathrooms, and anywhere you do a lot of reading or paperwork need the good illumination of task lighting. If you don't have much space, fit a strip light above your workspace or under a shelf or cabinet.

Mood lighting. Control the lighting and you can control much of the mood in a room. The same table lamp that provided bright light for reading can also create an intimate area for entertaining.

THE LIGHT CHOICE |

Chandeliers can range in style from traditional to modern. Typically, they are used to define dining areas. They also make small spaces, such as an entrance hall, feel spacious and grand.

Lamps instantly add color, interest, and mood to almost any corner. The lampshade's color, fabric, and shape will affect the amount and quality of the light you get. A shade may be colored, semi-opaque, or opaque.

making a fresh start

Making the living room in Hilary Offenberg's apartment unforgettable was a different kind of design assignment from the ones I usually take on. The room wasn't unattractive; it just held a few too many memories. Hilary lost her husband to cancer a few years earlier, and he had spent many days there when he was sick. So, living in it, or even attempting to redecorate it, was more than a little uncomfortable for her.

With my own experience of loss, I knew that surrounding yourself with soulful yet subtle reminders can bring comfort and familiarity to a home. Hilary and I discussed how she wanted the new room to feel, and she showed me a trunk filled with mementos from her marriage. Like all of us, she needed to keep these meaningful pieces of the past in order to embrace the future. But she also wanted to make sure those elements were incorporated in a way that avoided turning the room into a shrine, so that she and her young daughter, Carly, could move forward.

With all this in mind, I began by giving the room's subdued palette of chocolate and charcoal the change it so badly needed: a sunny yellow coat of paint on the walls and a crisp white trim at the ceiling. I filled a glass lamp with shells and sand that Hilary and her husband had collected on vacations, and gathered framed family photos into monogrammed albums. Then I put the front page of a newspaper from their honeymoon under a protective sheet of Plexiglas on a white leather tray table and hung one of Hilary's pretty floral watercolors on the wall above it.

To make the room feel even more like Hilary, I added a floral area rug, patterned upholstery on the slipper chairs, and soft finishes such as buttery leathers. Beading punctuates throw pillows, ribbons soften ready-made Roman shades, and flowers and greens from Hilary's shop breathe new life into this fresh beginning.

THE CHALLENGE Brighten up the palette and the mood | Layer the space with happy memories | Create a place to make new memories | Enhance the feminine factor

BEFORE

turn up the feminine factor

too monochromatic

HAPPY MEMORIES | An inviting high-back sofa (opposite) sits beneath a family vacation photo that was blown up and framed as an artful reminder of the past. A large round table softens the corner and serves as a great surface for accessories. Ribbon detailing adds charm to ready-made Roman shades.

BEYOND WORDS | Feathers have been floating into the home owner's life since her husband's death—as if he were sending her messages, she says. A perfect white feather, framed and mounted against burlap (below), is a tender tribute. Topiaries and candles make the spot even more special.

"for a feminine touch, beading, sparkle, and pretty trim do the trick"

take focus off the tube

ante up the accessories

TAKE A SEAT | Leather and linen upholstery warm the space, and a pair of stools provide easy-to-move seating (opposite). Accessories came out of the closet and found a new home on the coffee table, along with a member of Carly's stuffed animal family.

CONVERSATION PIECE | A credenza (left), painted black, anchors the flat-screen monitor and houses DVDs and videos.

brushing up on paint

FINDING A PAINTER

I recommend hiring a professional if your budget allows, especially if it's an architectural space such as a stairwell or high-ceilinged area, or a room that hasn't been painted in a long time and needs a lot of prep work.

When you're interviewing and getting bids, ask to visit some recent jobs. Set a schedule, define the scope of the job, determine who pays for all materials, and establish cleanup requirements.

If you're going to brave a paint job yourself, start with a smaller project and follow some of the tips on these pages.

The best thing about painting is repainting. It's by far the most inexpensive, immediately gratifying, and versatile decorating option available. Paint can be changed as quickly as it's applied, so don't worry about your indecisiveness or mistakes. And besides, there are ways to sample your shade in advance.

Choosing your colors. The only reliable way to view a color, whether it's a paint chip, a fabric swatch, or a carpet sample, is in the room where it will be used. I often paint large four-by-eight-foot boards—kind of like oversize swatches—that I buy at art-supply stores, with the colors I'm considering. I bring them to clients' homes so they can live with them for a few days, from sunup to sundown. All color changes, sometimes dramatically, depending on the light. That dark green area rug you loved in the bright light of the carpet store may look muddy, almost black, in your study.

Finishes. Most paints come in at least four or five finishes. For fine woodwork or moldings, I like the richness of a semigloss paint, in either oil or, better still, acrylic, which is easier to work with and to clean up. Both look beautiful and withstand chips.

Flat or matte finishes are best for walls with imperfections. They're easy to touch up but a bit more difficult to wipe down, so they're not good for a bathroom or kitchen. For those rooms, and for areas that get lots of traffic, try an eggshell finish (it can be washed and touched up) or satin, which offers a warm finish that is scrubbable (perfect for crayon mark removal), though touch-ups tend to show.

"highlighting the woodwork adds contrast, dimension, and soul to a room"

Supplies. Invest in quality materials—paint, paint rollers, brushes, and even drop cloths. They make a huge difference in how quickly the job goes and in the final finish. Cheap paint doesn't cover well, particularly in richer colors, and inexpensive brushes and rollers make the work harder, especially if you're using oil-based paint. Poor-quality plastic drop cloths tear easily, don't soak up spills, and can be slippery underfoot.

Prepping and priming. This is the step everyone rushes through, but that's not a good idea. If you take the time to prep the walls properly, your painting job will be much easier. Wash woodwork and walls to remove grease and dirt. Fill any holes or chips, and sand so you have a smooth surface to work with. Give the walls a final wipe with a damp cloth to remove any dust created by sanding. Take the time to tape around the trim and edges, and tape over or remove switch plates and light fixtures. Then roll on a coat of primer; if you're applying a dark color, ask the paint store to tint it toward the color of the room.

Once you've got the primer on the walls, apply the first coat. Paint the ceiling first so you don't end up leaning on the walls in an attempt to get up there later. Start at the top of the walls and work down. Follow the instructions and allow the paint to dry between coats; expect to apply at least two top coats, especially if you're using a dark color.

SWATCH WATCH

You can have paint matched to almost any color you're considering simply by bringing a fabric swatch or tearsheet to the paint store. But even if it's computer matched, you should still test out a quart on the walls before buying all the paint you'll need. What's great when it's the size of a vase may look overdone when it covers four walls.

home rules
creating a grand scheme

GARDEN VARIETY | Bringing plants and flowers, like these stems of vibrant purple allium (opposite), into a room adds an ever-changing supply of seasonal accents and good color lessons.

1 Don't be afraid to experiment with colors. Sometimes it's the only way to find out what colors you really love and can live with.

2 Try out my rule of four: One color, top to bottom, can be a bore, two might work, three can be interesting, four adds up to a rich, sophisticated scheme.

3 Your clothes closet often knows best. If you feel comfortable wearing a particular color, you'll probably feel comfortable living with a shade of the same color.

4 Paint is cheap and changeable, and it creates a rich result.

5 Try out your paint colors in the rooms where they'll be used before you make an all-out commitment.

6 Remember three things if you're going to paint it yourself: prep, prep, prep.

7 To play it safe, keep walls and major pieces neutral, then add color in the details. A patterned pillow is a lot less risky (and a lot less permanent) than a set of boldly upholstered dining chairs.

8 Unify your fabric and paint story. Collect all the pieces of the puzzle on a "story board" to see if you like the mix before you play the decorating game.

9 When in doubt, men's suiting colors such as camel, navy, gray, and crisp white are reliable choices.

10 Use lighting to create mood and influence the colors in your space.

3

Something for Everyone
Family Rooms

Welcome to the coaster-free zone, where games are played on the floor and forts are built with the sofa cushions. The place where your latest read rests on the coffee table, where you organize your weekly movie night, where you come to curl up by the fireside and guests are expected for wine and cheese.

This all-American room enjoys many a moniker, everything from den to great room to laid-back living room. Whatever it's called in your home, it's the catchall place where you all gather and live most of your collective life.

The key to designing a successful family room is to keep comfort at the forefront. Think simple and organized, so that each activity has its place: books on bookshelves, toys in a chest, and CDs and DVDs stacked neatly in baskets, boxes, or drawers.

This is also the put-up-your-feet place, so it makes sense to arrange the room around a large seating area. If you're starting from scratch, this should be your first purchase, whether that means an overstuffed sofa, two smaller pieces, or an arrangement that includes a mix of sofas and chairs.

Chances are, all furnishings in this room need to work overtime, so think handsome, homey, and hardworking. Finishes and fabric choices should be durable and, better still, washable. The point of this room is to enjoy yourself and the memories made here, without having to worry about the care of, or wear on, the furniture. Slipcovers—especially those made of machine-washable cotton—can be lifesavers; whether you're buying a new sofa or sticking with your old one, consider having a set made. A combination of wood floors and area rugs works well with furniture such as a coffee table or ottomans that can be moved out of the way or climbed on.

Most of us watch television in this room, and I'm all for it. But unless your set is the latest in technology, it's best kept behind closed doors.

This is also the room in which to incorporate your family's personality by breaking out your framed photos and showing off your collections. Make it cozy and inviting by draping a beautiful blanket over the back of the sofa and using easy-to-change pillows as interesting accents. Let the purpose of this all-purpose room focus on family.

"today's family room is the new living room"

ten questions to ask yourself
all in the family

HAVING A BALL | A kitchen and dining area open onto the family room (opposite). Floor-to-ceiling bookcases in warm wood tones display collectibles alongside an extensive library that includes handy homework references.

1 What's the purpose of this all-purpose room? Do kids play here or is it more for formal entertaining?

2 What kind of feeling do you want—handsome library or homespun hangout?

3 How much seating do you need? Where will the sofa have the best view?

4 Are you plugged in to all of your electronic needs (computers, music, movies)?

5 Does the room need to work as a home office? Does homework happen here?

6 Is this a spot for a small happy hour? Or are you planning for party central?

7 Ottoman or coffee table? Feet up or fancy? Does this piece need to move easily?

8 Have you got lighting in the right places? Overhead or lots of lamps?

9 Traditional or modern? Would you consider playing the sofa against type—a traditional piece in a modern setting, or vice-versa?

10 Is it a TV-guided room? Do you want it to be?

MODERN LUXURY | Tufting creates pattern and dimension on a sofa. On this fresh take on the traditional Chesterfield (above left), it offers a nice juxtaposition to the sofa's contemporary lines. Tufting interrupts patterned fabrics, so solids are the best choice.

TRADITIONAL AND TRUE | This cross between a classic square-armed Knole and a tuxedo sofa (above right) has clean lines that work well in almost any decor. Its casual cotton denim upholstery can be dressed up or down.

PLAIN FABULOUS | A tuxedo sofa with tufted detail and multiple cushions offers a clean contemporary line in a laid-back linen (left)—a comfortable and timeless selection for almost any room. A neutral fabric choice is a natural backdrop for easy accessory updates.

the best seat in the house

For most of us, a new sofa is one of the largest and most important furniture purchases we'll make. Regardless of your price range—whether you're buying one off the showroom floor or having one custom designed and built—it always pays to shop prepared. Have the dimensions of your room in hand. Try out cushions made with different fillings. Is the arm height right for you? How about the height of the seat? Check the workmanship: Does the sofa talk back when you sit down? Are the seams straight and finished off well?

Fabric facts. Find out what fabrics are available and in what price categories. Ask about durability and how easily they can be cleaned. (Generally, each fabric has a cleaning code label that tells how to deal with spots and stains.)

Frame-up. For me, top-of-the-line construction means eight-way hand-tied coiled springs; this minimizes the chances that the piece will warp. But other constructions are also good; the main thing to look for is stability. Sofas should be heavy and solid; just make sure the frame is made of kiln-dried hardwood that's both glued and screwed together.

Cutting costs. For the best deals, go the semi-custom route—choose a sofa from a large retailer, a catalog, or the Internet, then pick a fabric from one of several offered by the manufacturer in a range of prices. With custom sofas, you get furniture tailored exactly to your dimensions and finishes, and you can use any fabric you like, but they cost a great deal more and generally take much longer to deliver, sometimes several months.

THE WELL-CUSHIONED LIFE

It used to be that all sofa cushions were filled with down—soft, yes, but they require constant plumping. However, a filling of synthetic and down retains its shape longer than all down and is softer than all synthetic.

Seat cushions should be 24 to 26 inches deep; anything deeper will be fine for the tallest family members, but others may need an extra pillow behind their back to feel comfortable.

a good space becomes a great room

Jenny Lumet is a contagiously funny, soulful drama and theater history teacher with an impressive heritage: Her father is film director Sidney Lumet, her mother is author and historian Gail Buckley, and her grandmother is actress Lena Horne.

She's also a busy mother who needed help making her family room work better for her. The open-plan space, with its combination kitchen and living room, had plenty of personality, but it needed some grown-up style. A few years after the family moved in, the room still felt unfinished—it was a catchall space that just wasn't coming together.

Jenny's furnishings consisted of some interesting flea market finds and collections, but they weren't arranged in any particular way. The walls were painted a kind of uninspired white, and the slouchy sofa was facing a wall. With posters for art and no window treatments, the room needed to tell a better story.

We started by painting the walls a warm sand color. Then the floor plan got a new orientation to define the space: A tailored sofa, in a much-improved location beneath one of the large windows, now anchors the room. It faces a classic ottoman that doubles as a coffee table. A yellow chaise rests comfortably in front of another window, a sunny spot for reading or daydreaming.

Jenny's personal collections, mounted in museum-style cases and frames (found in catalogs), hang on either side of the sofa. Blue silk curtains and a blue-green rug frame the seating area, creating the sense of a soothing sanctuary.

In the old plan, kitchen and family room merged into each other. A simple but effective change is a new half wall that visually separates the two. As a final cheerful touch, the blond wood kitchen cabinets were painted white, and their interiors got a coat of robin's egg blue to cozy up to the curtain color.

THE CHALLENGE Make the space feel lived in, pulled together, and personal | Incorporate collections | Define the open space by creating distinct areas | Treat the windows and lighting to some bright ideas

BEFORE

windows should get dressed

shutter the clutter

SOFA SO GOOD | In the new floor plan, the sofa faces into the room (opposite). Its natural linen upholstery gives it a tailored look. Two charmingly mismatched lamps and tables create a symmetry; the glass lamp is dressed for the occasion in one of Jenny's necklaces. Store-bought drapery panels get a personal touch with rows of African beads found at a flea market.

SHE SHELLS | Jenny's love of the sea is reflected in a framed engraving of coral-colored scallop shells and the opal shimmer of a vintage sixties lamp (below).

"family memories should fill the halls and walls of your home"

ROOM WITH A VIEW | A half wall was key to giving the kitchen an identity as a separate space (opposite). The television should be hidden in this kind of open room, so we tucked Jenny's into a hip-height cabinet that sits against the new wall. It's now the perfect height for viewing, and the cabinet doubles as a serving area. New pendant lights and barstools give a more sophisticated look to the counter where meals are served.

SOMETHING BLUE | The plain kitchen cabinets got a fresh coat of white paint (left), and the backs of the glass-front cabinets went robin's-egg blue to set off Jenny's simple white china and pick up the curtain color. New knobs update the old cabinet, a quick and cost-effective change that adds to the kitchen's custom look.

blond is bland

BEFORE

the slouchy sofa won't stand up to style

dressing up
your windows

INSIDE MOUNT The term for a window treatment that's contained within the window frame. It always looks neat and tailored; it doesn't hide molding or window detail, but it does conceal unsightly panes.

OUTSIDE MOUNT Commonly used for curtains, with the rod hung above the top of the window frame. I prefer mounting the curtain rod as close to the ceiling as possible—it will make your ceilings appear higher.

CURTAIN PANELS These should extend from the height of the ceiling to the point where they just skim the floor. (Allow an extra inch in your measurement for windowsill clearance.) Each should be at least 12 inches wide and extend no more than 3 inches over the window when it's open.

SHADES Windows can be notoriously uneven, so measure the height on both sides and the width at the top and bottom. Measure each window separately, and to the nearest one-eighth of an inch; use a metal measuring tape for the most accurate reading.

Who would voluntarily sign up for something called a treatment? Sounds too much like a tricky medical procedure. I find that window treatments are the biggest headache for people because they assume they'll have to deal with yards and yards of elaborate fabric and complicated hardware. But consider this: When it comes to windows, simple is always best. Choose a tailored look and you won't go wrong. The window and the view are just as important as what decorates them.

Redefining custom. With all the customizable ready-made options available today, there's no need to spend a lot of money on true custom curtains. If you can handle a tape measure, you can order from a specialty store or a catalog. Select simple linen, cotton, or wool panels and hang them from rings on a wood or metal rod. Go for a tailored look with flat Roman shades, natural woven shades, or wood blinds with contrasting tape; ready-made bamboo shades and Roman shades in natural linen are my no-fail favorites.

Do it yourself. If you're handy with a sewing machine or a glue gun, you can do the customizing yourself. Lengthen a ready-made curtain by attaching a band across the top or a deep hem in a coordinating or contrasting fabric. (Picture a strip of chocolate velvet at the base of a linen panel.) Consider sewing several panels together to create a subtle striped effect. Edge a plain Roman shade with ribbon trim from the crafts store. Treatment complete.

FLAT-OUT FAVORITE | A store-bought linen Roman shade in Hilary Offenberg's apartment gets a custom look with the addition of bands of contrast ribbon trim (above left). This neat, tailored option works well in both classic and contemporary settings and is readily available in sizes that fit a wide range of widths and lengths.

GOOD WOOD BLINDS | Wood blinds like the ones used in Jerry O'Connell's living room (above right) come in a variety of stained and painted finishes; the addition of ribbon tapes covers the workings and finishes the look. They tend to be used in more casual settings such as family rooms and work especially well in bedrooms and bathrooms because they can admit light and still offer privacy.

A CERTAIN CURTAIN | The fabric, the rod, and the architecture of the room are the major components in curtain choices. You can dress up a simple fabric or store-bought panel with beading, buttons, fabric cord, or tape (left). Curtains work well on their own; over a shade or blinds, they create a layered look that also helps regulate the light.

picture this: arranging art

Want to create a great photo op for your walls and halls? Start by having the proper picture hooks, a hammer, a level, and a tape measure. Then follow these tips:

Plan ahead. Figure out your arrangement before you start banging holes in the wall. Move your frames around on a large piece of kraft paper, then trace their outlines onto the paper and tack the paper on the wall where you'll be hanging the art. You can also work out an arrangement directly on the wall using blue painter's tape.

Stay in line. Align your frames along at least one grid—at the top or bottom for a contemporary look, at the center for a more traditional treatment.

Mix or match. You can unify your arrangement by using the same matting and frames for all your pieces, or by choosing all vertical or all horizontal shapes. For a mix and match look, find frames in different styles and sizes, and try mixing horizontal and vertical shapes; sometimes an uneven pattern can be more interesting than a precise grid or lineup. Pinpoint the center of the wall and position your main picture there; it should be at eye level, about 66 inches from the floor.

Get artistic. For a classic, art gallery look, convert your color photographs to black and white or sepia at the local photo store, then frame them uniformly and simply.

GOLD STANDARD | The graceful line of a camelback sofa (opposite) is mimicked in the symmetrical arrangement of modern abstracts, 18th-century engravings, and a richly detailed vintage sunburst mirror. The gilt frames unite the pieces and blur the decades between them.

FILM NOIR | Jerry O'Connell's collection of family photos was converted to black and white and blown up to create a gallery-type display on a hall wall (above). They're all arranged in black frames with crisp white matting and placed about 8 inches apart.

focus on mantels

NUMBERS GAME | A parade of white pottery (above) takes shape in multiples, showing that grouping like items, colors, or shapes creates a good focus.

MIRROR MIRROR | A round mirror contrasts with the strong horizontal line of the mantel (opposite). Clear glass hurricane lamps on either end create an elegant symmetry.

The fireplace: symbol of hearth and home, focal point in any room—and a major decorating challenge for most of us. Displaying treasured objects or collections is a great idea, but the trick is to edit them carefully. As a rule, an assortment of well-placed accessories on the mantel creates more fire than a single statement above it. Here are some ideas:

Even is out. Lots of little items—photographs, flowers, candlesticks, potted plants, figurines—can look like clutter. Make groups of uneven numbers and you've created instant eye appeal from across the room.

Simple is in. Stick to simplicity on large items and repetition in shape, color or subject on small ones. A single beautiful mirror or a grouping of small leaning framed images always looks great.

Fill-ins. Alternating larger items with small objects brings the eye in for a closer look.

Hearth healthy. Avoid a black hole between fires—a stack of new firewood is far prettier than yesterday's ashes. In warmer months, conceal the firebox with a screen or an interesting object. You can also fill the space with a stack of papery white birch logs, or replace the grate with a wicker basket.

BOXED SET | A handsome display of leather and wooden vintage boxes holds memories of the places where they were found (above left). They take on added dimension on the sideboard in a living room, layered, stacked, and mixed with a collection of shells.

WHITE ON | A creamy patina unites a mixed assortment of vintage ironstone and French Mocha-ware pitchers, bowls, and cake plates (above right). The collection is functional as well, swinging into action as serving pieces or as centerpieces filled with flowers or fruit.

BOLD REFLECTION | A sitting room shows off its boldly framed group of antique Federal convex glass mirrors (left). The repetition of strong black lines and reflective surfaces makes a powerful statement by repeating and grouping like items.

showing off
your collections

Whether you have a taste for beautiful coffee table books, silver boxes, vintage dishes, or old advertising signs, building collections can enrich your decor and your family relationships. Whatever you choose to collect should be something you love, not something that necessarily has monetary value.

The art of display. Showing off your collections to their best advantage requires a few rules:

- Three or more like objects create a more purposeful and powerful statement than just one or two.

- Grouping different items by color can also create a cohesive collection—all white pottery, mirrors in gilt frames.

- Three or more collections in a room will distract attention from one another. Your home may wind up feeling more like a store.

Living out loud. Collections don't have to hang on walls or live out their lives in glass cases. A wonderful set of mix-and-match floral china or antique wineglasses can liven up a simple meal. An album of historic photographs or an architectural fragment set out on the coffee table will intrigue visitors. Vintage silver or wooden boxes make excellent homes for your jewelry.

easy updates

BLANKET STATEMENT | Throws are versatile, to say the least. A woolen blanket (above) adds color and texture to an all-white sofa, and an invitation to nap regardless of the season. Treat yourself and your sofa to seasonal slipcovers. This sofa (opposite) is dressed up in its all-white summer version. A new throw on top adds just the right swirl of personality, and it reverses for another quick change. All it took was a yard-and-a-half remnant of an expensive designer textile at a bargain price.

in an hour

- Refresh the sofa by fluffing pillows and flipping the seat cushions.

- Split your pair of matching night tables in the bedroom and move one next to the family-room sofa.

- Rearrange accessories on a tabletop; group like items.

- Decorate the mantel.

- Stow the kids' toys in stylish baskets.

in a day

- Edit down your furniture—take at least one piece out of the room.

- Lay down a new area rug in a different color or shape.

- Buy a throw for the love seat in a completely different pattern or color.

Move your furniture

- Move your furniture around—try the ottoman in front of the fireplace; put a side table between your two chairs.

- Use a screen to section off a part of the room to create interest, a personal space, or a hiding spot.

- Toss some pillows on the sofa and chairs.

in a weekend

- Check out the flea market for good-looking side tables.

- Choose a different fabric for an upholstered piece.

- Reframe your photographs or artwork.

- Organize your books by color; add decorative items between them on the shelves.

- Paint the room a fresh color.

"make every nook feel gracious, inviting, comfortable, and warm"

home rules
make everyone happy

STAND AND DELIVER | A chrome pole lamp (opposite) is an enlightened choice in this seating area. The individual lights can be moved as needed, whether for reading, television, or family talks.

1 Comfort is key in the family room because so much important downtime is spent there.

2 Buy your sofa first; it will set the style and scale of all your other furnishings.

3 If your family room gets constant use, especially from children, choose the most durable—and washable— upholstery fabrics you can find. Cotton and linen are good choices.

4 This is the perfect room in the house for comfortable seating and family mementos.

5 A chest of drawers or a low cabinet is a solid option for toy and CD storage.

6 Use ready-made or built-in bookshelves where possible. They add both storage and beauty.

7 Admit it, the family room is for watching television, so find a strategic spot for comfortable viewing and enjoy.

8 Side tables are fun to look for and easy to find—and they can ride home in the car.

9 Use table and floor lamps to add atmosphere to the room. They do a better job than overhead lighting.

10 Use the entire room; a comfortable chair tucked in a corner can create a reading nook.

4

Living Large
Small Spaces

Space-challenged rooms have earned an unfortunate reputation, but the truth about them is that they can be the most charming. We just need to think about them as special, not small. That nook just big enough for floor-to-ceiling shelves and a comfy chair can check in as the library you've always longed for. Even a closet can be turned into a home office with a simple desk and a wireless laptop. It's all in how you look—or look again—at the small stuff.

More than in any other room, the trick in small spaces is to use what space you have wisely; to play up any qualities it may have, such as beautiful moldings, a fireplace, or a pretty view; and to choose furnishings and storage solutions that are in scale, that function efficiently, and that are pleasing to the eye. A small space might not require lots of furniture, but what it does have has to work overtime. The simple addition of one fantastic piece of furniture can change the whole feeling of a small room. Look for furnishings

that can do double duty or that are made expresssly for small spaces—a coffee table that can be raised to dining table height, an end table with generous drawers for storage, a sofa that's slightly scaled down so that it fits without feeling Lilliputian.

And because your small space isn't all that many square feet, this may be the perfect time and place to try out that paint color you've been shy about committing to or to hang a few rolls of that patterned wallpaper you've had your eye on for a while.

No matter what the size of your space, living gracefully is the ultimate goal. If this isn't a call to redecorate, make it a call to clear the visual clutter. That doesn't mean turning your interior into a minimalist showroom; it does mean eliminating everything that interferes with your comfort and tranquility.

If you still feel uncomfortable, try reducing the number of pictures on the wall, or the collectibles on the side table, until you've created a place to rest the eyes. Stash bedding, books, and toys in baskets, under the bed, or behind a screen. A small room is a perfect opportunity to balance beauty and necessity, and that's the biggest news of all.

"the biggest surprise
in a small space lies in its
built-in intimacy"

ten questions to ask yourself
expanding your horizons

SPACED OUT | An unused corner of Paige Davis's master bedroom (opposite) was transformed into a cozy seating nook with a screen. Carter Oosterhouse of *Trading Spaces* custom-painted the screen in the same sleek color scheme of blood orange, chino, and chocolate used in the pillow fabrics.

1 What's the purpose of the space? Are you trying to make it serve too many functions? Can you simplify?

2 Can you edit down to only what you need? Ask yourself the tough questions, and find the middle road somewhere between restrained and overflowing.

3 Can you use pieces you already have for more than one purpose? Will that dining chair also work as a desk chair? Can that stool serve as a bedside table?

4 Want to make a big statement? This might be the spot for a bold paint job or great wallpaper.

5 Can you create a focal point to lead the eye away from the space limitations—a decorative headboard, an oversize painting, or a beautiful chandelier?

6 Are there places to store surface clutter out of sight, like cosmetics, magazines, CDs, DVDs?

7 Are you thinking out of the box—literally? Is there a nearby closet or hallway, or a garage, basement, or pantry that can handle some of the room's storage overflow? How about going vertical to free up floor space?

8 Could that closet function better as a mini home office? Sometimes, giving up one space to create another makes more sense.

9 Is there a view that you can draw into the room? Is there a way to minimize window treatments to let in as much light as possible?

10 Are you taking advantage of all the space, such as shelves over doors, underbed storage?

big ideas for close quarters

Everyone—even an authority on makeovers like Paige Davis, former host of the TV series *Trading Spaces*—needs a makeover sometime. The one-bedroom, one-bathroom apartment she and her husband, actor Patrick Page, share was a mix of hand-me-downs and holdovers from apartments past, filled with potential but lacking their personality and charm.

Paige had always wanted a mix of modern and rustic, combined in a way that was sleek but still warm and comfortable. She was looking for a new layout with room for entertaining, for a home office, and for a guest bedroom. Because the space was small, I didn't want to put up walls to achieve all this.

I left the kitchen and dining area open to one another but linked visually by the clean lines of wood cabinetry and shelving. The result is airy, comfortable, and inviting. The dining area addresses Paige's taste for a rustic and modern mix: The table base, made from real tree branches, is topped with glass. A vintage chandelier creates an interesting contrast to the contemporary dining chairs.

Changing the configuration of the furniture also opened up the apartment and helped define and separate the different areas. Before, when you entered, your path was blocked by the back of the sofa. Now the new seating runs beneath the windows, making the space feel larger. The modern sofa can be easily rearranged for a different look. Sculptural wood stools, which can be clustered to make an impromptu coffee table, continue the rustic theme.

I brought in a new sofa bed and positioned it at right angles to the walls to give Paige a multipurpose office/guest room/media room. Floor-to-ceiling curtains close off the entire area when guests come; the same curtains hide a pair of his-and-hers office spaces from view.

To maximize space in the master bedroom, an unused corner was treated to a pair of new chairs, creating an intimate area for the couple to enjoy at the end of a busy day.

THE CHALLENGE Define inviting spaces for work and play | Marry modern and rustic styles | Link the kitchen and dining area naturally and comfortably | Maximize the space in the kitchen with new storage solutions

BEFORE

this kitchen has no character

white's not right

FORM AND FUNCTION | With a nod to restaurant style, new open shelving creates easy-access storage (opposite). New white solid-surface countertops look crisp, clean, and modern. A multipurpose island provides storage and acts as a serving station and a place for informal meals. A limestone tile backsplash defines the working areas around the sink and stove. More like furniture than fridge, a commercial glass-front refrigerator (below) casts a glow that contrasts with the warm color of the cabinetry.

"play up luxe over little with lush fabrics and furnishings"

FLEXIBLE LIVING | The living room/dining room opens onto the multipurpose guest room/media room/study (opposite). To break up the space but still provide maximum flexibility, floor-to-ceiling curtains on a track serve as a soft "construction-free" wall.

IN THE STICKS | The country-meets-contemporary look of the new canopy bed is a clean take on the traditional four-poster (right). Its tall, spare lines make the room feel airy and outdoorsy. Pillow fabrics in blood orange, chino, and chocolate inspired the rest of the room's color scheme.

this thing's gotta go—seek sleek storage

couch is creating great-room gridlock

BEFORE

BEFORE

more mix and match than master suite

SHEER GENIUS | The clean line of Paige Davis's curved glass coffee table (above left) creates a grand illusion in this small den. Because it's see-through, it keeps the look of the room light and open.

NEW VIEW | Strategically placed mirrors can double a room's size and light. This decorative vintage piece in Kirstie Alley's narrow laundry room (above) reflects the light from the sunny kitchen just outside the door.

SCREEN SAVER | This sculptural wooden divider (left) serves a tall order: It adds an aesthetic note to an entry hall, where it also functions as a temporary clothing rack and conceals bags and other clutter.

make every inch count with…

Color. A monochromatic scheme, especially in a lighter hue, will keep your small space feeling big. Warm it up with texture in cozy rugs, fun pillows, and a few touches in an accent shade that shows off your personality.

Pattern. Generally, it's better to minimize the amount of pattern in a small space. But sometimes the same allover pattern on walls and upholstery can actually make boundaries seem to "vanish."

Screens. Screens can divide a single space into separate areas, allowing one room to serve many purposes. Tuck the sofa bed behind one by day; hide a galley kitchen after it has completed its cooking duties; conceal a less-than-tidy work area from view. You can even cordon off a corner to hide exercise equipment.

Furniture. Regardless of your decorating style, keep the lines of your furniture clean and crisp. Avoid overstuffed arms on chairs and sofas; straight arms and armless options take up lots less space.

Storage. If closed storage options are at a minimum, think creatively about adding smart "out in the open" solutions: meant-to-be-seen cloth-covered baskets stacked on bookshelves, pretty hampers that hide the laundry without a linen closet or serve as toy storage, mini stacking drawers to hold sewing supplies, paper-covered document boxes for photographs and letters.

SMALL TALK

• Consider replacing your bathroom door with a pocket door that slides into the wall instead of opening into the space.

• Rearrange furniture so that it isn't lined up against the walls, as if it were under house arrest. This leaves a hole in the middle of the room that you can't use.

• Add casters to any piece of furniture that you need to keep mobile.

• Use smaller-scaled chairs that can easily be moved around the room or drawn up to a coffee table for impromptu dining.

• Build shelving all the way up to the ceiling or above doors or windows to maximize storage.

grand plan for a one-room wonder

My first project for *The Oprah Winfrey Show* was the tiniest studio apartment I'd ever seen, in a historic brownstone on an idyllic Boston block. The place was long on charm, but it was suffering from a severe storage shortage, and the cramped kitchen was tripping all over itself. It needed some imaginative ideas to make it live larger and to bring out its innate appeal.

I completely understood why the home owner, Claudia DeFino, had fallen for every last inch of the 319 square feet, although her friends and family thought that her five-paces-wide space might have been a big mistake. But all it takes is one detail—like those incredible soaring 18-foot ceilings—to make even the smallest place feel palatial. The original wide-plank wood floors, loads of natural light, and the historic setting made me fall in love with the space as well.

Claudia had exactly four pieces of hand-me-down furniture to her name and stacked crates that served as storage. Her six-by-six kitchen had a microwave oven teetering at the edge of the sink and a dishwasher door that collided with the cabinetry on the opposite wall.

To unify the apartment and make it appear larger, I kept the color palette simple, using moss green and sand. I designed a floor-to-ceiling built-in wall unit for the longest wall to take full advantage of the apartment's distinctive height. The closed cabinets make convenient storage, while open shelves at the top keep it feeling airy. The whole unit frames a sofa bed that pulls out to become a queen-size bed. Shelves on either side double as night tables, and a large mirror above makes the space seem twice as big.

The other furnishings are light and move easily in and out of the picture. The coffee table is also a wine rack, and a wicker basket serves as both side table and storage for bedding. Opposite the sofa, a clothes closet doubles as an entertainment center, showing off the TV only when the doors are open. Each precious inch is accounted for—with room to spare.

THE CHALLENGE Make maximum use of architectural charm | Create as much storage as possible | Keep the overall look sleek and chic "make a sweeping statement by working the room floor to ceiling"

BEFORE

wanted: big-time storage solutions

a futon isn't furniture

BEFORE

this is more alley than galley

HEIGHT OF ELEGANCE | Two store-bought curtain panels for each window were stitched together to create the perfect length for the grand ceiling height (opposite). A table that opens to store folding chairs sits beneath a chandelier that defines the eating and entertaining area and makes the space even loftier.

PETITE PUZZLE | To avoid losing valuable storage space in the kitchen, stock cabinetry was extended to reach the ceiling (right). Wallpapering the cabinets' recessed door panels gave them a custom decorative touch. Small-scale appliances, such as a stainless dishwasher drawer and a built-in microwave oven on the opposite wall, get the job done in half the space.

two for one: double-duty ideas

TO FLIP FOR | Almost any tabletop can work as a desk, whether a nightstand or a kitchen table with a drawer to stow paperwork and pencils. This clever side table (above) becomes a desk just by lifting the lid. The underside was made into a beribboned cork board, perfect for keeping to-do lists, pictures, and notes.

TWO FOR ONE | Hanging a soft wall (opposite) is worlds easier and less expensive than creating a construction site. A floor-to-ceiling curtain can pull off the perfect game of hide-and-seek in just about any space. Paige Davis's media room lost a two-by-eight-foot slice along one wall but gained his-and-hers home offices.

Everything in a small space should serve more than one purpose—even the room itself.

Choose furniture that works harder. A drop-leaf table can stand against a wall until it's opened up for party time; a small-scale sofa bed can hide its full-size bed by day; end tables may include wine racks below; a coffee table can double as a dining table. Use a large ottoman to conceal storage beneath a lidded top; find a coffee table with a lower shelf to store wicker baskets. Place a wide console table behind the sofa that can double as a desk; a set of three nesting tables takes up the space of only one; use a trunk in a kid's bedroom and store books, toys, or bedding inside.

Make better use of your rooms. Hallways can be great places for shallow shelves or cupboards for table or bed linens. Let the computer or writing desk share the guest quarters; add a soaring wall of bookshelves to your dining room and you've got a library as well. A mudroom, basement, or garage can serve as pantry space or storage for rarely used kitchen appliances.

Change a room's identity. Is your child leaving the nest? Turn his room into a home office with a sofa bed or into the sewing room you always dreamed of. Maybe you have no use for your formal dining room, as was the case with one of my clients. I turned her dining area into a media room filled with cozy love seats and ottomans (perfect for feet-up movie viewing); her old sideboard turned out to be the perfect place to store the DVD player and CDs.

"it's curtains for the home office—
revel in the big reveal"

"carve out a corner where you can be inspired"

home rules
how less becomes more

COMMAND CENTRAL |
Cook up an office in a corner of your kitchen (opposite) and you can keep on top of paperwork and family meals at the same time. All you need Is a bulletin board and an attractive chair—perfect for Mom to keep track of ball games and school schedules.

1 Edit, edit, edit. Decide what you love, what you need, and what works, then remove everything else from the room. Stay focused.

2 Be brave with color. Sometimes a bold monochromatic statement can do big things for a small space.

3 Go vertical—use every inch of height you have: cupboards to the ceiling, shelves above doorways.

4 Make a painting, a mirror, or a fantastic light fixture the focal point of the space.

5 Dress windows simply and make the most of the natural light available. Just because a room is small doesn't mean it has to be dark.

6 Create a place for everything, from television remotes to house keys. Don't let tabletops and counters get out of control.

7 Be a stowaway. Search for stylish options to house everything you don't want to see all the time. A handsome chest of drawers or a sideboard can store more than just clothes or dishes.

8 Look for furniture that's hardworking enough to serve at least two purposes.

9 Keep the floor as un-cluttered as possible. Use a large rug to unify the space.

10 Smaller-scale appliances and furnishings can make your space feel grander.

5

The Right Recipe

Kitchens

Ladies and gentlemen. Families of all ages. Cocktail-party singles: Welcome to center stage, the heart of your home. The kitchen is the gathering place where we eat, entertain, do homework, pay bills, visit with friends—even cook. The room has come a long way from its purely utilitarian past. Today's version combines the tradition of yesterday with the high-tech gear of tomorrow.

The old basics—cabinetry, appliances, and counter-tops—are basic no more. The marketplace is just about overflowing with products that answer to every style idea and price point, from traditional to ultramodern. Yet with all of the options available, keeping it simple is still my best advice. My favorite recipe is clean, painted Shaker-style cabinets, subway tile on backsplashes, and marble or stainless steel countertops, stainless appliances, and

polished nickel handles and knobs. I'm not a fan of lots of fancy tile work or kitchens that are decorated around a theme. When I've moved away from this classic model, it's been with the certainty that the look wouldn't get dated anytime soon. Whatever your particular taste, remember that you'll probably be living with your choices for many years; outside of high-tech advances, what's new in decorating isn't always best in this room.

Most of us don't have the luxury of creating a new kitchen from scratch. But even if all you're doing is updating, it's possible to get a fresh new look simply by changing just one or two things: Paint the cabinets a clean white semigloss; change the hardware; treat yourself to a new stove, dishwasher, or refrigerator (or all three) in stainless steel or white; or add tile to the backsplash. Then show off your personal style with wall color, dishes, art—even place mats and napkins can reflect your style.

Together with new materials and appliances, the other major change in kitchen design is the room's relationship to the rest of the house. What used to be a closed-off space now often opens directly onto many other rooms, so it has to work decoratively with those spaces. We live much more casually than we used to. Most guests come in through the back door and straight into the kitchen. What better reason to make it an invitation to welcome a fresh perspective.

"a blend of informed and creative kitchen decisions creates a successful recipe"

ten questions to ask yourself
what's cooking in your kitchen?

WARMING TREND | Wearing a chef's hat at home has never been easier. Stainless steel stoves (opposite) modeled after restaurant designs have been scaled down for the home and made more user-friendly than their professional cousins.

1 What's your kitchen's mission? Is it just for cooking, or is it for dining and family gatherings as well?

2 What are your goals—update or renovate? Are they realistic in terms of budget and time?

3 Are you a serious cook? Do you need professional-grade appliances? A marble countertop for baking? An oversize freezer?

4 Do you prefer open or closed storage? Are you neat enough to let it all show?

5 Do you have enough counter space? Can you stow away small appliances?

6 Do you entertain a lot? Need extra storage for dishware and glassware?

7 Is this the family office? Do you need a place to do paperwork, bills, and homework?

8 Do you have sufficient light to work by? Or good light to dine by?

9 Want to eat in? Would a table with chairs be best, or are you a more casual island-style family?

10 Are the cabinets set up for maximum storage? Could a few drawer dividers double the duty?

looking beyond cooking

Creating a kitchen that is part of what's going on in the rest of the home gives it great energy. Actor Jerry O'Connell's kitchen was cut off from his apartment and it wasn't working for him. It had old cabinets and white appliances, and a small room adjacent to it served only to provide a home for a discarded Denny's booth.

The first step was to break down the wall between the two rooms, which not only doubled the size of the kitchen but opened it up to the living room. The single window in each of the original rooms worked better as a pair.

Inspiration for the decor came from the many open kitchens in restaurants that were some of Jerry's favorite haunts. The room took on plenty of warmth with the addition of a dark wood floor and a sculptural central light fixture on a dimmer. The cool stainless steel table, indoor-outdoor chairs, and glass-front steel-clad cabinets work well with the

BEFORE

This wall should fall

open up the possibilities

Carrera marble countertops. The table, conveniently set on casters, can move easily from prepping island to fancy dining.

Jerry says the makeover made him over. At his first post-makeover party, he brought out coasters—and even asked guests to take off their shoes.

STEELING FROM THE PROS |
Sleek, steel-clad cabinetry and stainless appliances combined with dark, wide plank wood floors set an industrial tone (opposite). Sandblasted glass cabinets will conceal not-so-neat items.

THE CHALLENGE Create a comfortable place to socialize | Keep it masculine but functional | Open the kitchen to the living space

"folding storage ideas in every corner stacks up to efficiency"

easing the space crunch

Let's be honest—no matter how big your kitchen, you can always use more space. There's an easy way to get it without ripping up the room. Remove the extras. Clear the counters: Organize your papers and mail in baskets, or file them away. Clean out your cabinets; throw out the spices you never use. Put away appliances you don't use on a daily basis; come to terms with the fact that you're never going to use that fondue pot—ever. Here are some other ways to help expand the space you have:

- Over-the-sink cutting board and basket

- Wall-hung dish racks and shelves for everyday dishes and glasses

- Drawer organizers that eliminate the need for a knife rack

- Appliances and small electrics—microwave oven, toaster, radio—mounted under top cabinets

- Cabinet dividers to organize your glasses and dishes

- Pull-out shelves that keep small items from getting lost in the back of the cupboards

- Overhead pot rack

- Pot-lid holder hung inside a cabinet door

- Small-scale rolling cart that serves as a mini island

- Large trash basket mounted on wheels

- Hinged shelf mounted at the end of a counter, which can be folded down when not in use

SEE WORTHY | Inset organizers in stainless steel (opposite) give equal-opportunity access to items at the front and back of the cupboard; shelves move out as the doors are opened. Rotating spice racks (above), also in sleek stainless, are as practical as they are handsome.

california dreaming

Kirstie Alley has a wonderful Mediterranean-style home, but the large kitchen was last renovated two decades ago and it was definitely time for a change.

The house is buzzing with people and a parade of pets running in and out nonstop. Like so many of us, Kirstie not only cooks in her kitchen but also works and entertains in it, and her kids do their homework there. The space was poorly laid out to serve as the heart and hub of the home, the countertops were in bad condition, and the island was covered in impractical tiles. Well-organized areas for all the family's activities needed to be defined so that everyone and everything had a comfortable place.

The kitchen also had poor access to the outdoors—the only way to get there was through a door inconveniently located outside the room. As a result, it felt closed in, and Kirstie dreamed of extending it to incorporate the patio.

We worked together to create a list of design elements and styles that she wanted in the new room. Although we were gutting much of the space, I wanted to preserve the old bones and history of the house. We started with tiles in a vibrant apple green, in a shape that was reminiscent of 1920s architecture. (I'm usually a white-tile guy, but I wanted to use the color Kirstie has always loved.) Cove molding in a toffee brown balances the color and highlights the edges and details of the design, creating a one-of-a-kind pattern.

The vaulted and arched ceiling is covered in mini mosaic Carrera marble tiles, and the countertops are finished in marble slabs to match. A new stainless steel stove and hood are flanked by cabinets that echo the shape of the original cabinetry.

French doors now open from the kitchen to the patio. Kirstie and her family can finally take full advantage of the warm California sun.

THE CHALLENGE Create a better layout for a multipurpose kitchen |
Respect the original architecture | Connect to the outdoors

BEFORE

banish the blues

tile not in style

BEFORE

let's catch some more rays

THROUGH THE LOOKING GLASS | Kirstie used to keep her beautiful porcelain and ceramic dishes in storage boxes. Now these special items are displayed in glass-front cabinets lined in French pink-and-ivory-striped wallpaper (right). Keeping the room's architectural details whenever possible was an important goal. Some original curved cabinetry, still in place on one of the walls, was used as a template for custom-built new cabinets, like those over the countertops.

OPEN INVITATION | French doors create convenient access to the patio from the kitchen (opposite). Comfortable seating areas were created with outdoor furniture that looks like wicker but is crafted from a man-made resin that's impermeable to the elements. The custom cushion fabric is fade resistant and can also withstand a shower.

"indoor decor ideas
play outside, too"

easy updates

SUBWAY PLATFORM | A shelf above a subway tile backsplash (above) adds an artful upper deck for displaying a collection of cake plates and framed prints—and clears the counters, which now work better as well-needed workspace.

GLASS ACT | A slim set of shelves stacks up as a clearly creative use of space and as a visually pleasing place to stash glassware (opposite).

in an hour

- Put all your counters in order.

- Put cooking utensils in a pretty pitcher or a piece of vintage pottery.

- Clean up your counters with a shiny new set of canisters.

- Cheer up a dark corner with a bouquet of flowers.

- Replace old curtains with wood blinds.

in a day

- Refresh a tired sink with a new faucet.

- Replace cabinet pulls with new ones in nickel or stainless steel.

- Paint the inside of glass-front cabinets.

- Put up a simple display shelf for your cookbooks or collectible dishware.

in a weekend

- Revive a wood floor with enamel porch paint.

- Install undercabinet task lighting; kits on the market make installation quite easy.

- Change the bulb in your overhead fixture to give you a softer, warmer light.

- Put a dimmer on the fixture above your dining area.

- Have the cabinets painted by a pro, or do it yourself with the help of a home-improvement store.

"every corner of the kitchen
calls for creativity"

recipe for success

COUNTER INTELLIGENCE | This buffet-ready counter (opposite) is a little higher than standard, hiding clutter around the sink from view and creating the perfect place to pull up chairs for a casual meal.

1 This is often the busiest room in the house, so keep the design clean and cleanable.

2 Look past trends. If you don't live in Tuscany, don't do a Tuscan kitchen.

3 Full-height backsplashes add a luxurious look; white subway tile is my forever favorite.

4 Natural stone countertops can be expensive, but they're worth the investment in terms of beauty and durability.

5 Hardwood floors really stand up to the comfort test.

6 Stainless steel appliances will update any decor, from traditional to modern.

7 Keep it organized— find room for everyday essentials such as papers, bills, shoes.

8 For a more spacious look, turn your upper cabinets into open shelving.

9 Create a statement with light fixtures that are decorative as well as functional.

10 Add personal touches with kids' artwork, colorful pottery, flowers on the windowsill.

Rest and Relaxation
Bedrooms

Go to your room. Make your bed. But this time make it really special. You deserve to surround yourself with comfort and beauty. Why do we so often leave this room until the end to decorate—shouldn't it be the first? A well-designed bedroom is the best possible space to wake up to. It greets you as you open your eyes and embraces you as you drift off to dream. Surprisingly, the bedroom is one of the easiest rooms to decorate. Choose your bed first, and choose it carefully, both for looks and for comfort (a simple fabric-covered headboard, for instance, is a favorite because it looks luxurious, is great for reading in bed, and doesn't have to cost much), and position it to take advantage of the best view. How you dress the bed can make this focal point all the more personal and appealing. You can keep adding and subtracting elements such as pillows, duvets, and throws to create different looks.

The rest of your bedroom furniture doesn't have to be a set of anything; unmatched pieces are always more interesting—a modern triple dresser and an antique armoire, for example. If you need your night tables to offer storage, try a small-scale dresser and a vanity table or an oversize round table.

Small luxuries count for a lot in this room—good advice for your guest bedroom as well: extra pillows on the bed, candles, a stack of good books, pretty flowers on the nightstand, a throw for afternoon naps, iced water and glasses. This is also the place for personal items such as photographs and souvenirs. If you enjoy watching TV in bed or having a movie night in the bedroom, keep the set behind closed doors when it's not in use for the most soothing effect.

Framing the bedroom windows with curtain panels creates a soft but tailored look when flanking a Roman or roller shade that lifts or lowers at night. Finally, choose your favorite paint color — this is a great place to paint the ceiling the palest shade or hue.

And the rest, is rest.

"make every night feel like a night in a fantastic hotel"

ten questions to ask yourself
how do you sleep easy?

SWEET DREAMS | A comfortable mattress is your first priority (opposite). If you haven't bought a new one in the last ten years, it's definitely time. Educate yourself about fillings, springs, and manufacturing processes. Then visit a reputable dealer and try out mattresses until you find one you like—remember, everyone's definition of comfortable is different.

1 Do you like a bright, sunny welcome in the morning, or is dark and enveloping more your style?

2 What color makes you feel calm? What hue on your bedroom walls would be soothing and tranquil?

3 How do you like your linens? Are you tucked in and tailored or more down-filled and fluffy?

4 How about waking up to something soft and warm under your feet? Wall-to-wall carpet or an area rug? Or are wood floors still right?

5 Can you make room for extra pampering—a full-length mirror, a chair so you can sit and put your shoes on?

6 Would you like a bed to climb up into—or keep it on the down low?

7 Can you fit a bench, chair, or ottoman for extra seating in an unused corner? A basket for magazines or books?

8 Do you read in bed? Can you install bedside sconces? Do you have room on your nightstands for reading lamps?

9 What do you keep by your bedside? What you keep at arm's length may help determine the size of night table you use.

10 Do you like watching television in bed? Is movie night your idea of a weekday vacation?

from dreary to dreamy

After more than twenty years of marriage, and more than their share of decorating differences, Sharon and Phil Rybarczyk were out of ideas for the master bedroom in their home in suburban Illinois. Her orange-and-green sponge-painted walls were vetoed even before they could dry; his do-it-yourself project in the adjoining master bathroom had been on hold for five years.

They wound up living with a green monster of a bedcover that poorly concealed the dip in the middle of their hand-me-down mattress; a dated gold bedside chair; a filing cabinet that didn't quite work as a dresser; and cardboard boxes that served as closet organizers. A brick wall stood where a would-be fireplace never blazed, and the outdoor balcony was an unused bonus in need of a furniture fix. The couple found themselves racing out of the room the moment they awoke and waiting until after dark to duck back in. It was time for a little design intervention.

Sharon and Phil needed a fresh new style, something that would allow them to truly enjoy the whole room as a peaceful retreat. We started by painting the walls a rich cinnamon color and getting them a real bed and new linens; an upholstered headboard and footboard, plus a pair of night tables, enhance the overall style. Removing an old sofa from the middle of the room created space for a generous seating area, with two love seats facing each other across a simple round coffee table. The windows were transformed by luxurious silk curtains. The balcony, now complete with table and chairs, is the perfect place for the couple to read the paper and share their morning coffee.

An especially memorable aspect of this makeover was framing an anniversary card that Phil had given Sharon and surrounding it with petals taken from a dried bouquet of roses, a keepsake from their fifteenth wedding anniversary. It was a final touch to a stylish retreat that welcomes the couple at the end of the day.

THE CHALLENGE Design an overall overhaul | Combine romantic decor with clean lines | Define a conversation area | Make the deck a part of the plan

"an inviting corner for
conversation or alone time"

camouflage
paint job
needs to take
cover

BEFORE

say good-night
to tired bedding

WARM AND INVITING | The new sleeping area (opposite) is framed by luxurious silk curtains and a pair of matching night tables. New linens and an upholstered headboard and footboard contribute to a comfortable, pulled-together look.

PLEASE BE SEATED | Two love seats (left) were upholstered in a neutral fabric so accents can be easily changed if the home owners choose to create a different mood. Cinnamon-colored walls and accessories in shades of red, orange, and brown add depth and richness to the room. An étagère creates height, so that everything isn't on the same level.

sleeping in style

PILLOW TALK

A mix of interesting pillows on the bed dresses up the room.

• Twin bed: Place a standard sham in front of a standard pillow, and finish with two decorative pillows.

• Full- or queen-size bed: Start with two standard or European shams and place two standard pillows, side by side, in front of them. Finish the look with two or three decorative pillows.

• King-size bed: Start with three European shams, side by side; place four standard pillows in front of them and finish with three to four decorative pillows.

CHEAT SHEET

THREAD COUNT: The number of horizontal and vertical threads in one inch of fabric.

TYPES OF WEAVE
Percale: smooth, closely woven fabric that looks the same on both sides.

Sateen: lustrous fabric with a thick texture and sheen.

Jacquard: intricately textured fabric with a design woven in.

Wake up—it's time to get dressed. When choosing bedding, have some fun: Play florals against checks, try linen against silk; go all out with throws and bed skirts and pillows, or be sleek and minimalist with a quilted duvet. Have one look in summer, another for winter. Don't be afraid to experiment, even changing styles when you change the sheets.

Sheet story. I prefer a very high thread count, but sheets with thread counts between 200 and 400 will serve you well. Sheets blended with polyester may make you feel hot and uncomfortable, so my advice is to opt for a natural fiber, such as silk, linen, or cotton. Cotton is generally the fabric of choice; Egyptian and pima cotton both have a beautiful softness, superior durability, and luster, in percale, sateen, or jacquard weave. Shop for your sheets at a store where you can touch them and examine the workmanship to ensure that the finishing details, like hems and corners, are neatly done.

Cover-up. A down or synthetic-down duvet is an easy, one-step way to dress—and make—your bed. It adds height and plushness, but it may be too hot to sleep under. A blanket, bedspread, or coverlet looks tailored and neat when it's pulled taut and the top sheet is folded down at the top. A throw tossed casually at the foot of the bed adds texture, color, and interest; it's also great for those times when you want to curl up and read the paper or watch TV.

TEST PATTERN | A mix makes the match with a modern woven canvas and walnut headboard against vintage-inspired paisley velvet pillows and a goatskin night table (above left). A custom striped wool area rug in warm oranges, reds, and blues pulls the color play together.

BED HEAD | A fabric-covered or slipcovered headboard is a good-looking, classic, and affordable way to achieve a finished feeling without buying a new bed set (above right).

TINT HINT | Pick up accent colors from the room for your bedtime story. Layer up the color connection with a mix of interesting pillows, patterns, and textures, along with a blend of hues like these blues (right).

Pampering celebrities is something Ellin LaVar does very well. This time she treats herself to her own retreat

MAKEOVER
MAGIC

beauty rest

Ellin LaVar, hair stylist to the stars, self-made CEO and queen of her own empire of best-tressed products, wanted more than a bedroom—she wanted a personal haven. Like so many of us, she dreamed of having a special place to return to after a long day at work.

Ellin couldn't define her style, but she knew she wanted it to feel luxe and European. Fashion books from the 1930s and 1940s inspired the entire makeover. After studying the dressing rooms of Paris couture houses of the period, I decided to give her plain, boxy bedroom a little French lesson.

One look at the small space with its matching set of cherry furniture, not to mention a home office and a treadmill, and I knew I'd have to start from scratch. Achieving the glamorous look Ellin wanted would take lots of lush textures, soft colors, and period details.

First, we said good-bye to the exercise equipment, the paperwork, and all the dark furniture, including the four-poster bed, which made the small room look even smaller. Then we covered the parquet floor with plush, wall-to-wall carpeting in an ivory color that sets off accents in every shade of Ellin's favorite color: purple. A new headboard, upholstered in lavender linen, a lilac linen bedskirt, and a purple throw turn the bed luxurious. Patterned silk damask pillows stacked on crisp white sheets complete the couturier look.

Two matching lilac night tables offer open storage, keeping the tops free for pretty personal statements. Above them, a pair of sconces adds a Parisian flavor. The opulent gray walls and luminous silver gray wallpaper on the ceiling were enhanced with white baseboards and crown and picture-frame moldings for a touch of history and instant age. A bit of trim worked magic on ready made Roman shades. Now Ellin has a made-to-measure dressing room of her own.

THE CHALLENGE Create a restful retreat out of a plain room | Find furnishings that don't crowd the space | Add architectural interest to the walls | Play with a purple palette

BEFORE

a bed shouldn't overpower a room

hair-raising clutter

BRANCHING OUT | On an ornate marble-topped French chest (right) a pair of polished-nickel table lamps, ceramic coral branches, and a ceramic urn form a tablescape of elegant symmetry. A piece of contemporary wall art strikes a balance between modern and historical.

FRENCH DRESSING | The room's ceiling was skim-coated with plaster and covered with silver paper to add glamour and an illusion of height (opposite). The upholstered headboard takes up far less space than the old four-poster. Next to the bed, a little painted stool is pampered by a French silk scarf. On the window, Roman shades get a lift from the addition of gray grosgrain ribbon trim and stationary purple silk drapery panels frame a glorious view of Manhattan. Even the radiator gets a pretty decorative cover.

"make a fairy-tale bedroom come true with lush color and period detail"

"wake up to bedding that inspires a great day and good night"

easy updates

in an hour

- Buy a candle with a scent that transports you.

- Bring home fresh flowers you deserve to wake up to.

- Organize the night table and tuck clutter out of sight.

- Move out the exercise bike and create a place to read.

- Explore some paint colors that will change the look of the entire room.

in a day

- Treat yourself to new linens, pillows, or throws.

- Give old photos new frames to wake up memories.

- Arrange pictures on the wall to create your own gallery.

- Add a soft bedside rug to pamper your feet every morning.

- Buy a full-length mirror.

- Purchase new bedside lamps for a bright new outlook.

in a weekend

- Paint the room a color that inspires you.

- Install wood moldings to add architectural detail.

- Slipcover the headboard to add fresh style.

- Move in a writing desk and buy pretty new stationery.

- Create a reading nook with a comfortable chair, ottoman, and table lamp to finish the room.

BEDSIDE MANNER | A quilt or cotton matelassé coverlet makes for an easy-to-make bed (opposite)—it's light, comfortable, and tailored, and can be dressed up or down. Think of making the bed in the same way you would put together a great outfit: Gradually layer colors and patterns in pillows, blankets, or duvets for an interesting but not too busy look. Finally, add a knit throw, as you would toss a sweater over your shoulders. A bench at the foot of the bed is a beautiful and functional finishing touch, a place for extra blankets or magazines and books. A warm area rug layered over a wood floor (above) is a great way to wake up to comfort and sink your toes into the day.

hollywood handsome

BEFORE

plain boring

not very Jerry

Actor Jerry O'Connell had a typical guy's bedroom: bare and functional, furnished with a mix of hand-me-downs. The closets were stuffed and disorganized, and the overall look was far too plain for his big personality.

Bedrooms need to be inviting and intimate, and this one definitely wasn't. Since Jerry likes grays, browns, and tans, we used that palette, along with red and blue accents, as a basis for creating a warm, masculine-looking room. We installed dark wood floors, then painted a narrow white border around the perimeter to add character. The walls got a coat of dark charcoal paint, instantly upping the sophistication factor. Curtains in chocolate velvet contribute softness and luxury to the room.

A new bed with a leather headboard is reminiscent of a chair in an Ivy League men's club. Placing it at an angle instead of beneath the window gives it more presence; behind it, a large plant softens the sharp corners with a touch of green. Crisp white sheets with dark brown edging and a cashmere throw complete the bed's fresh, tailored look. The new night table—actually a round dark wood dining table—holds vases, books, and a bedside lamp. Now Jerry comes home to a new take on old Hollywood glamour.

MAN'S WORLD | The walls got a dark coat of charcoal (opposite), instantly upping the sophistication factor. Chocolate velvet curtains add a layer of luxury and softness to the room, while emphasizing a sense of intimacy.

THE CHALLENGE Create a cool and comfortable new style | Add personality along with function | Go for a grown-up look

"classic good looks make for
movie-star style"

children's rooms:
a place of their own

As children grow, their rooms go through many phases, from newborn nursery to toddler playroom to teenage hangout. Let your children participate in the design decisions when they're old enough—kids not only have ideas of their own, but they'll derive a sense of pride and accomplishment from knowing that they contributed. Consider some of these decorating ideas as well:

- Plan for more storage than you think you need. Baby things are small, but children's clothing and school-paper stacks grow pretty quickly.

- Try a vintage child's desk or a vanity as a crib-side night table.

- Grass-cloth wallpaper and cork tiles won't show push-pin holes and are durable, good-looking choices for walls. Cork provides excellent sound insulation, too.

- Hang hooks, Peg-Boards, or even coat racks for jewelry, hair ornaments, mementos.

- Wood floors with area rugs are easier to maintain and change than wall-to-wall carpeting.

- A slipcovered headboard can make a transition with a child as he or she grows up; it's soft, and it's easy to wash.

- Add a chair rail, or a shelf about 18 inches from the ceiling, all around the room for displaying collections.

- Old sports memorabilia make nice lamps and accessories for young fans.

- Chalk up a section of the room (even the back of the door) as a place for some blackboard paint—it can keep messages and play dates in plain view.

- Personalize pillows with a monogram or iron-on initials. Or hang a varsity-size fabric-covered letter above the bed.

KID STUFF | A room that combines sporty but stylish ideas is easy to agree on (opposite). Dad's old bunk trunk (perfect for tossing in toys and equipment) is covered with a collection of team and travel stickers; a rustic-looking bed frame is tops for sleepovers or for sharing a small room. A vintage desk is a handsome homework spot—very cool-looking when paired with modern chairs and a shaggy rug.

home rules
wake up to wonderful

FEELING QUILTY? |
Matelassé, also called double cloth, is an elegant upholstery-weight fabric that's a classic and crisp choice for bedding (opposite). A slightly cushiony finish gives it the look of a tailored quilt. It's a wonderful year-round choice as a coverlet and mixes easily with other textures and textiles.

1 Make the bed luxurious and inviting. Buy good sheets and pillows, and always have a cozy throw on hand.

2 Serenity is key, so keep wall color soothing and the trim crisp.

3 Have lights on dimmers, and shades or curtains that are easy to raise and lower to enjoy the morning bright or savor a good, long night.

4 Create a reading nook with a chair, an ottoman, and a good lamp. Keep a stack of magazines and books on hand.

5 A mix of bedroom furniture is far more interesting. Separate a suite; night tables don't have to match.

6 Use an armoire or a cabinet to conceal the TV when it's not in use.

7 Keep work and workouts out. If you do paperwork here, make sure you can put it out of sight before you go to sleep.

8 If you have the luxury of a big closet, hide your dresser in it. Your room will be prettier and more spacious for it.

9 Choose versatile furnishings for your children's rooms that can be adapted to different stages of their life.

10 Make your bed every day. You'll feel organized and accomplished right from the start.

7

The Ultimate Retreat

Bathrooms

It's time to come clean. Nowadays we're spending more quality time than ever in the bathroom. Where else in the house can you make a grand escape to be happily alone to coif, calm, and collect yourself? Grown up and well groomed, the bathroom should be the most restful and relaxing room in the roost.

The great thing about a bathroom makeover is that you really can make a few small changes like new paint or a new faucet and sink for a minimal investment and give the room a complete and stylish new look.

Whatever you have in mind, first take stock of what you need to do. Ask yourself: Who will be using the bathroom? How much use will it get? Do you want to create the luxurious feel of a spa? And, of course, how much do you want to spend?

There are so many styles, fixtures, and materials that it helps to have a plan at the beginning of any project, big or small. Just remember that your new design should be easy to clean and easy to maintain. As when making an important sofa purchase for the living room, you should also start with the big stuff. The sink, tub, and tile are the major players and in my opinion always feel right in white.

The simplicity and charm of vintage styles can look as fresh, timeless, and clean today as they did years ago. Many new bath designs have called on the past for their good bones. If you're are lucky enough to inherit an original fixture or tile in good condition, consider leaving it in place or reglazing it to its original finish (this may be less expensive than a replacement).

Remember that floor tiles need to be durable and slip-resistant, while wall tiles don't; since ease of cleaning is important for both bath and shower walls, something with a shiny glaze is better. Lighting fixtures and faucets can be something new in a nickel or an antiqued brass finish or something vintage found at a salvage shop or flea market. When you consider your paint and linen choices, you may want to choose a soothing color such as a pale blue or green. Bolder color choices are better for a powder room or rooms that are used less often, like a guest or half bath.

For an easy update, just add a few thirsty towels, a narrow shelf with a row of scented candles, or a new shower curtain and rug. Even a small indulgence can mean a big change in the bathroom.

"count on updates to recharge and renew your bathroom *and* your well-being"

ten questions to ask yourself
what's your idea of luxury?

BOWLED OVER | Place extra hand towels in a decorative bowl (opposite) and bath towels in a bin or basket. It's a colorful way to decorate, and you always have a spare towel within reach.

1 Renew or redo? Do you actually need to gut the space to get what you want, or can you simply pamper the place a bit?

2 Do you have room for a separate tub and shower?

3 How do you light it right? Could you use close-up lighting around the mirror? How about some mood lighting (table lamp or dimmer)?

4 His and hers? Are double sinks right for you?

5 Pedestal sink or vanity? Do you need extra storage space? Or are you working with a small room that calls for smaller-than-standard fixtures?

6 Do you have a lot of cosmetics and skin-care products that need a home? Will a single medicine chest do?

7 Do fixtures need a fix? Are they the wrong color? Are they cracked or discolored?

8 Could a quick fix brighten the day? Take stock of your towels and see if they should be freshened up.

9 Would you like to upgrade the shower? How about two showerheads or a hand-held shower? Built-in seating?

10 Do you have room for a small seat or bench or extra towel bars and shelves?

Paige Davis's dark, divided bathroom trades two spaces
for one luxurious plan

getting the spa treatment

BEFORE

what lurks behind the curtain?

did someone turn out the lights?

My take on bathrooms is that they should be as light, bright, and airy as possible. The one in Paige Davis's apartment was dark and outdated, and oddly divided into two little rooms: a sink, toilet, and bathtub in one, and a second lone sink in the other. Dark countertops and plain mirrors felt a bit too "came with the place" for Paige's savvy personality.

The first step was to unite the two rooms to gain a few precious feet, which brought me to my biggest challenge: working the plan around the existing plumbing, which couldn't be moved. (Note: Always check this out before you start on your dream plan.)

Inspiration for the color scheme—serene blues and greens—came from Paige's sea-glass collection. Mini mosaic glass tiles reminded her of vacations past, so we used them as a shimmering backdrop to the shower-bath combination, then threw in an oversize, wall-mounted rain showerhead, in chrome, for over-the-top luxury. One great sink is better than two. Ceiling lighting on a dimmer goes from soothing to more soothing.

Small changes, such as bars of fine-milled soap and new towels stacked on three reclaimed timber stools, add to the escape quotient. Paige can now truly feel as if she were coming home to her personal spa after a long day on the set.

THE CHALLENGE Modernize a dark, dated bathroom | Bring in serene spa influences | Create a soft, restful lighting scheme

WATER WORKS | A countertop of honey-colored natural limestone, which matches the floor, sets off a white rectangular undermount sink (above left). The statue is a find from Paige's travels.

SPA-WORTHY | In a small bathroom, a European-style hinged glass shower barrier (above right) is a better choice than a curtain or sliding glass door. It keeps the splash at bay but lets the light in and makes the shower feel more open.

CASE CLOSED | Replacing a small linen closet with a glass-front cabinet (left) created storage for towels and bath and beauty products and freed up precious space in the bathroom. The new cupboard repeats the rich cabinetry used in the apartment's kitchen and dining room (see pages 88-91).

"imagine the bath as your own
piece of the sea"

easy updates

in an hour

- Buy new towels, shower curtain, and bath accessories.

- Replace hardware on the vanity with new or vintage glass or nickel knobs.

- Add personality to the room with fun accessories, such as a mint julep cup or an old sports trophy to hold make-up brushes, or a scallop shell to hold soaps.

- Get a bathtub tray to hold your book while you soak.

in a day

- Hang an old apothecary cabinet or shelves for storage or displaying things like vintage glass bottles or candles.

- Paint a wood vanity white, ivory, dark gray, or green.

- Consider removing the old medicine chest and hanging a decorative mirror in its place.

- Find a replacement for your old faucet at the home-improvement store or flea market.

in a weekend

- Paint the room a soothing shade, such as pale green, gray, or sea blue. Just a hint of blue tint on the ceiling can refresh the whole room.

- Have the tile regrouted, or if you feel ambitious, do it yourself. A fresh coat of grout can seal old imperfections and make the tiles look new.

- Have your stained or old porcelain tub resurfaced. The coating restores the shine and lasts from three to five years.

THE LITTLE LIST OF LUXURIES

Lush soaps and bubble baths

Natural sponges

Pretty bottles to hold shampoos

A beautiful container for your toothbrush

Monogrammed towels

A medicine chest mirrored inside and out

A plush rug

A new showerhead

A stool or bench

Dimmers on light fixtures

Time for yourself

Need some quick changes for the bathroom?
A whole new look can be achieved in less than a weekend

fast-fix bath

BEFORE

time for new towels

sink the black fixtures

already in place, including floor-to-ceiling Carrera marble tiles that gave it the sleek "hotel" look the actor likes. But the black toilet and sink had a little too much style—old Las Vegas to be exact.

Bathroom fixtures are fairly universal—if you take one out, you can usually find a replacement at a home improvement store. This means you can make significant changes in a day or two—instant fun and almost instant gratification. We started by swapping the two black fixtures for timeless white (one of my favorite choices), then added a sophisticated chocolate wood vanity with a clean-lined stone top to match the marble floor and walls.

The old faucets were traded in for modern nickel ones that enhance the updated look. And finally, we tossed out Jerry's mismatched towels, replaced them with plush all-white ones, and settled them into their own handsome new armoire. All in a day's work.

Actor Jerry O'Connell's bathroom wasn't as "bachelor" as the rest of his apartment, but after redoing his kitchen and bedroom (see pages 108 and 136), we just couldn't resist the challenge of doing a one-day, construction-free update. The room serves both the master and guest bedrooms, and some nice features were

THE CHALLENGE Do a makeover with minimal time, construction, and cost | Replace old linens and add sleek new storage

REFLECTED GLORY | Think outside the medicine chest when decorating the bathroom. A large mirror, meant to be hung in an entryway or living room, works well as a decorative addition over the sink (opposite). It also visually doubles the size of the small room.

"make taking a shower as luxurious as a scrub in the tub"

home rules
pampering 101

SHOWER POWER | Simply changing your showerhead, faucets, and fixtures can make an old shower feel new. If you're redoing the shower, consider adding an in-shower spa seat, a built-in shelf, or a soap ledge for extra convenience (opposite).

1 However small or extensive your update, keep it simple and soothing.

2 Show your pearly whites—white is always right for sinks, tile, and toilets.

3 A ceiling-mounted rain showerhead seems like a nice idea, but it's hard to get out of its way. Wall-mounted is much more practical.

4 If you want to wallpaper, do it in your powder room—there's no steam from the shower to worry about.

5 Use lighting to make the room more welcoming. Candles or a small low-wattage table lamp provides soft light for a relaxing soak.

6 Small luxuries mean a lot—plenty of good towels, nice soaps, a soft rug.

7 If you're short on storage space, look outside the room for solutions.

8 Carve out a space for seating—it's one of the ultimate comforts in a bathroom.

9 When it comes to bath accessories, skip the sets and look for great-looking vessels to hold everything from trash to toothbrushes.

10 Think before you replace old tile or an old iron tub or pedestal sink. You may never be able to replicate its charm.

Contain Yourself

Organizing

Ready. Set. Get organized. Putting your home in order involves everything from the relatively confined task of coordinating the chaos in your clothes closet to the adventurous undertaking of reorganizing or even rethinking each room. This isn't merely a once-a-year toss-out or tag sale but a way of living an orderly life on a daily basis, and of feeling a sense of well-being about yourself and your home. The rewards of creating an organized environment are a sense of peace and calm—and who doesn't crave that?

No matter how much space we have, most of us are in search of a little extra room in the closet or in the bathroom or a clutter-free zone to call our own. Cleaning up your act, even in the smallest rooms in the house, is an instant way of focusing your priorities. Removing and

discarding clutter or unnecessary extras cuts down on confusion, helps you focus on what's important to your life, and lets you be surrounded by what you love. Do you need all those old magazines? When was the last time you wore that dress? Be tough—the idea is to live with what you want, not everything that you own—but be fair. Try putting some things away for a while (nothing permanent—don't panic) and see if you still miss them in a month or two.

Throwing things away is only the first step; the next is to put systems in place that your family can follow and feel comfortable with. That means finding a sensible—and stylish—place for everything: medical records, bills, newspapers, laundry, kids' toys, house keys, photographs, family and school papers. Make sure everyone knows where everything goes, and get them to participate in keeping things neat and in their place. Imagine the emotional and practical payoff for the whole family—yes, even the pack rats among you.

When you look around your organized abode and everything is neatly tucked into its place, it's sure to clear your mind and spark your decorative vision.

"organization means finding the right place and space to put it all away"

ten questions to ask yourself
is there order in your court?

COLOR WORKS | Sorting clothes by color (opposite) not only makes for an orderly room, it will also make you feel like you're shopping in your own closet. And organization will soon begin to feel like second nature.

1 Are you a pack rat or just plain disorganized? Quantity of life is not quality of life—get to the bottom of the pile and decide what you really want to live with

2 Which room needs the most help?

3 Is your home office set up for maximum efficiency? Do you waste time looking for supplies, files, phone numbers?

4 When was the last time you cleaned out your clothes closets? When was the last time you wore that outfit?

5 What lurks in the attic? If you can't remember what's up there, you probably don't need it.

6 Are you keeping a gift that doesn't suit you? Can you pass it on to someone who might enjoy it?

7 Are your photos sitting in boxes? (They should be framed or put in albums.)

8 Can you carve out a space, however small, dedicated to specific needs (ironing, paperwork, homework)?

9 Are your bed linens still a set? Do your towels match? What about dishes and glassware?

10 Have the children outgrown some of their toys? Will some playthings find a better home with a favorite charity?

"storage containers come in all shapes and sizes—buy ones you'll always want to see"

clean up your act

For those of you who are trying to keep clutter at bay—and who isn't?—there really are solutions. Clear a date on the calendar and make it "moving day." Start with one room—any room. Set a realistic goal and give yourself plenty of time. You may be able to get only one closet done, but that could inspire you to move on to the rest of the house.

Value judgments. Once you've decided what you want to keep, separate those items into what you plan to use right now and what can be put away. Clearly label all boxes that are going into storage; if you have a lot of boxes, it's a good idea to number them and keep a detailed list of the contents in a notebook.

Stuff to go. Sort through all the items you've decided to get rid of and organize them into three piles: what can be thrown out (be ruthless—if the towels don't match and they're getting threadbare, get rid of them); what you can donate to a favorite charity; and what you want to sell.

Clutter to cash. Ebay is an excellent way to sell more valuable items. For everything else, consider organizing a tag sale. Entice your kids to participate: They can donate toys they don't use anymore, then take the proceeds from their sales and get something they really want. My nursery school teacher said it best: "Before you take out another toy, first put back the one you are playing with." We all knew just where everything was supposed to go. And so will you.

JUST CAUSE

Furniture, dishes, bed linens, and kitchen utensils can have a second chance if you donate them to any of a number of organizations that sell them to benefit charitable causes.

Many hospitals, smaller charities, and religious organizations run thrift shops. Some require that you bring all items, including furniture, to the shop itself. Others will pick up large items for transport. Call ahead and ask about their policy.

If you make a detailed list of the items you contribute and have a charity representative sign it, you may be eligible for a tax write-off at the end of the year.

HIDE AND SEEK | A stack of vintage boxes and suitcases store cufflinks, photographs, and CDs while the big baskets hide the weekly dry cleaning and ironing piles (opposite).

Finding a way to build some boardroom into the bedroom helps this home owner deal with the business of the day; it took less work than you might think

built-in beauty

BEFORE

closet alert: watch for falling objects

utter clutter

Finding space for a home office calls for ingenuity and the three rules of real estate: location, location, location. For celebrity hair stylist Ellin LaVar, the only available space was in an armoire in her bedroom, which spilled its contents over the floor like suburban sprawl. But she wanted to be able to retreat to her bedroom for some well-deserved down-time, and that meant the office had to be out of sight and out of mind.

How to hide the workspace when day is done was solved with built-ins (an ideal choice in small spaces). I created three of them behind new pairs of mirrored doors—one a compact home office, complete with a built-in desk and storage. (The other two hold her entertainment center and her clothes.)

I used cork on the inside of the closet doors and painted it the same shade of lavender as the inside of the closet itself. The corkboard displays Ellin's collection of inspiring beauty images from magazines, while a ribbon board allows invitations and keepsakes to be tucked away, too. Boxes on the storage shelves contain the clutter and the files. Task lighting—a slim strip light under the shelf above the computer—throws just the right light on the desk.

Just think: When you have a nice space, it could actually be a pleasure to draw up a chair and pay bills.

THE CHALLENGE Organize clutter and get more efficient | Hide the office away after business hours | Personalize a workspace

OFFICE MAX | Ellin's files are easily accessible; electrical outlets and an Internet connection are concealed inside the wall (opposite). Best of all, she can enjoy a work-free environment simply by closing a door.

"make the business of the day
a pure pleasure"

saving grace: preserving your memories

There's a fine line between keeping a memory and hanging on to all things sentimental. But tucking mementos into a drawer is not nearly as special as transforming a few of them into artful home accessories that you can enjoy every day.

School days. Kids' school papers and handmade items pile up quickly. Keep them in oversize archival envelopes, fabric-covered archival boxes, or labeled file folders and have your child choose a favorite at the end of each year. Frame the prized picks and hang them in a place of prominence.

Memory books. Scrapbooks are a great way to keep holiday photos and souvenirs—menus, postcards, invitations, ticket stubs. Do-it-yourself tools are readily available at crafts or specialty stores. Use an archival pen or permanent ink to date materials. If you aren't a crafts kind of person, slip items into a book with plastic or paper pocket pages.

Photo ops. Make color copies of your photos and let your children fashion framed collages of their favorites. Or help the kids create their own album or box of favorites. Have a piece of glass or clear plastic cut to fit a desk or tabletop; beneath it, slide school awards, postcards, letters, tickets to shows, or photos.

Child's play. Laminate a set of your child's paintings and use them as place mats, or use the many cute cups and small containers that children make in the early grades to hold paper clips, pencils, and erasers on your desk.

MEMORY LANE | A tray with a removable Plexiglas top holds a newspaper from Hilary Offenberg's wedding trip (above). Look for display cases, jars, or specially designed frames, such as collector's boxes (frames with open tops), to show off your mementos. You can even use a lamp base to display items like these beads from Jenny Lumet's family vacation (opposite).

Turning a closet full of opportunity into
a colorful collaboration

o is for organize

BEFORE

let's shed some bright on her topic

feels more hide than chic

After I'd done several makeovers on the show, Oprah asked me to step into her closet. Actually, it was three separate rooms of racks that had more than a few hang-ups. She asked me to think about a way to organize her wardrobe that would make it easier for her to get ready for the show each day.

Many questions came up along the way—some you can ask yourself if you're thinking of customizing or organizing your closet: How would the design make it easy to see every selection? Would there be space for packing? Where would accessories go? What overall design would represent beauty, quality, and functionality—and be fun to use every morning?

We decided to organize the closet by color and occasion (work, formal, etc.) so that all the contents could be seen at a glance. I wanted Oprah to feel as if she were shopping in her own boutique every day, so we created a large island in the center of the room to house all of her shoes and boots on open shelves. We kept the rooms' original leather floor and used a millwork style based on old English paneling that Oprah had chosen. The finish on the wood was kept light so that the clothes could take center stage.

Oprah's reaction? She turned to the camera and said, "America, this is a great way to live!"

THE CHALLENGE Organize on a grand scale | Create a space for everything | Brighten the morning routine | Make it easier to find exactly the right outfit

SHELF LIFE | Glass-front cabinetry allows easy viewing while protecting bags and hats from dust at the same time (opposite). Open shelving makes for quick access, and closed drawers are divided to contain accessories organized by category.

the new order

Calling your closets to order ensures that your rooms stay under control, too. Here are some of my favorite ideas for clearing the chaos out of the corners of your life.

In the clothes closet. Sort clothing by type—jeans, dress pants, dresses, suits—and then by color. Stuff purses and shoes with tissue paper to help them keep their shape. Fold all sweaters; they'll stretch and lose their shape on hangers.

Divide and conquer. Collect loose items such as scarves and socks in baskets and bins. Add shelf dividers to keep stacked items neat. Place hooks or a Peg-Board along the closet wall to hang belts, scarves, and tote bags. Place shoe racks on the backs of doors not only for shoes but also to hold small accessories. Put out-of-season items in storage boxes or suitcases and stow them on high shelves or under the bed.

Hanging on. Treat yourself to cedar or heavy wood hangers to help your clothes keep their shape and save you hours of ironing; the cedar will also keep moths at bay. Save cotton-covered hangers for delicate items. Double-hung rods are great space savers in a small closet; hang one rod about two feet lower than the first rod for shirts and blouses; the higher rod is good for out-of-season clothes. Vertical hangers for skirts and trousers are another way to save valuable closet space.

O, THE THINGS WE KNOW

Borrow a few big ideas and make them your own:

• Color-code your clothing—not only is it easier to find what you're looking for but it's a great system for keeping things neat. This is how the department stores stack the racks.

• A low bench or stool inside or outside the closet becomes a great space for packing or laying out your clothes for the day. It can double as a step stool for those hard-to-reach shelves.

• Look for store-bought shoe racks to line the floor of your closets.

• Add a light inside the closet—your things will never get lost in dark corners again.

GET IN LINE | A well-organized life starts the minute you walk through the back door (opposite). A space for jackets, sports equipment, outdoor shoes, keys, and even the dog's leashes keeps them in their place and out of the rest of the house.

"turn household hodgepodge into a clean scene"

home rules
sorting it all out

HORROR SHOW | Don't be overwhelmed by overflowing (opposite). Look to stores and catalogs filled with the stuff that organizing dreams are made of. Outfit your house with orderly options and storage solutions you can live (better) with.

1 Get organized today. It isn't a chore; it allows you to live with what you love.

2 Think creatively—you may find space where you least expect to, and solutions you didn't think existed.

3 Buy in sets. Matching hangers create more space in your closet; matching sheets and towels will make your organizing easier.

4 Be a basket case. I use them everywhere for everything.

5 Make it "pretty neat": If you like the way it looks you're more likely to use it, from vintage suitcases and hat boxes to leather in-and-out trays.

6 If you haven't used it, worn it, or seen it in a year, give it away.

7 Get everyone in on the act. Give kids their own laundry bag, toy bin, or sports locker.

8 Create a place for every thing. If something doesn't have a home, it's sure to get lost or become clutter.

9 Your mementos probably aren't giving you much pleasure in the basement. Choose a few, frame or display them, and enjoy them every day.

10 O.C.D.: Organize closets daily. In other words, if you take it out, put it back.

Resources

We would like to thank everyone who generously allowed us to photograph their homes and all the talented and dedicated people who worked on the makeovers.

(Where sources are not provided, items belong to home owner.)

Front Matter
PAGE 3 **blue glass vases:** Crate & Barrel, (800) 967-6696.
PAGE 5 **mantel:** Au Coin du Feu Ltd. (312) 850-2655.
PAGE 7 **for detailed information visit www.oprah.com** (search: jerry o'connell).
PAGE 10 **vases:** Bedford & Company, New York, NY, (212) 772-7000.

Chapter One
Inspirations
PAGE 25 **antique beads** (bottom center): Beads of Paradise, New York, NY, (212) 620-0642.
PAGE 28 **all items:** Yellow Monkey Antiques, Cross River, NY, (914) 763-5848.

Chapter Two
Color
PAGE 34 **silk pillows:** Crate & Barrel, (800) 967-6696. **silvered seashell:** Bedford & Company, New York, NY, (212) 772-7000. **throw:** Gracious Home, New York, NY, (212) 231-7800.
PAGES 36-39 **Benjamin Moore colors:** Classic—cream (Mayonnaise OC-85), camel (Tyler Taupe HC-43), white, and black; Modern—olive green (Green Grove 2138-10), sea blue (Gray Cashmere 2138-60), khaki (Shaker Beige HC-45), and rust (Boston Brick 2092-30); Garden—pale pink (Wispy Pink 2005-70), charcoal (Days End 2133-30), parchment (Mayonnaise OC-85), and silver (Ice Cube Silver 2121-50); Beach—navy (Old Navy 2063-10), white, sand (Shaker Beige HC-45), and orange (Fireball Orange 2170-10); Preppy—khaki (Yorkshire Tan HC 23), kelly green (Cactus Green 2035-20), pale blue (Bird's Egg 2051-60), and white; Sexy—lilac (Lavender Mist 2070-60), white, gray (Gray Cashmere 2138-60), and brown (Appalachian Brown 2115-10); Pop—hot pink (Red Tulip 2000-30), orange (Blazing Orange 2011-20), white, and linen (Shaker Beige HC-45); Handsome—navy (Old Navy 2063-10), royal (Evening Blue 2066-20), white, and black.
PAGES 40-45 **for detailed information visit www.oprah. com** (search: romantic room).
PAGE 40 **vase** on table, **ceramic vase, metal sculpture, smoky glass vases:** Pavilion Antiques, Chicago, IL, (773) 645-0924.
PAGE 42 **bowl and vase on mirrored table, table lamps, green suede pillows:** Crate & Barrel, (800) 967-6696.
PAGE 43 **decanter:** Pavilion Antiques, Chicago, IL, (773) 645-0924. **barware:** Crate & Barrel, (800) 967-6696.
PAGES 44-45 **plastic cube pedestals:** The Container Store, (888) 266-8246. **glass vase, carafe, coaster, dish, velvet pillow:** Crate & Barrel, (800) 967-6696.
PAGE 47 (bottom center) **lamp:** Gracious Home, New York, NY, (212) 231-7800. **vases:** Linens-N-Things, (866) 568-7378.
PAGES 48-53 **for detailed information visit www.oprah.com** (search: let the sun shine in).
PAGE 58 **orange and yellow vases:** Crate & Barrel, (800) 967-6696.

Chapter Three
Family Rooms
PAGE 64 (top right) **all items:** Yellow Monkey Antiques, Cross River, NY, (914) 763-5848.
PAGES 66-71 **for detailed information visit www.oprah. com** (search: jenny lumet).
PAGE 73 (top left) **all items: for detailed information visit www.oprah.com** (search: let the sun shine in). (top right) **all items: for detailed information visit www.oprah.com** (search: jerry o'connell).
PAGE 74 **engravings:** Reid and Wright, New Preston, CT, (860) 868-7706. **paintings** (Nicholas Howey), Dinaburg Arts, New York, NY, (212) 807-0832. **all other items:** Yellow Monkey Antiques, Cross River, NY, (914) 763-5848.
PAGE 76 **wicker urn:** Crate & Barrel, (800) 967-6696. **throw:** IKEA, (800) 434-4532.
PAGE 77 **cushions:** ABC Carpet & Home, New York, NY, (212) 473-3000.
PAGE 78 (top right, bottom left) **all items:** Yellow Monkey Antiques, Cross River, NY, (914) 763-5848.
PAGE 80 **chair, cushion, throw:** Yellow Monkey Antiques, Cross River, NY, (914) 763-5848.
PAGE 81 **fabric panel on sofa:** Scalamandré, (800) 932-4361. **throw:** IKEA, (800) 434-4532.
PAGE 82 **pillows, throw:** Gracious Home, New York, NY, (212) 231-7800.

Chapter Four
Small Spaces
PAGES 88-93 **for detailed information visit www.oprah.com** (search: paige davis).
PAGE 88 **glass vase, footedcompote in bookcase:** Crate & Barrel, (800) 967-6696. **leather box and snakeskin box in bookcase:** Barney's, New York, NY, (212) 826-8900.
PAGE 91 **serving dish and pitcher on island, bowls on bottom shelf, vase and pitcher on top shelf, dish on stove:** Crate & Barrel, (800) 967-6696.
PAGE 94 (top left) **box:** Barney's, New York, NY, (212) 826-8900. **tray:** Crate & Barrel, (800) 967-6696.
PAGES 96-99 **for detailed information visit www.oprah.com** (search: small-space makeovers).
PAGE 102 **rattan basket:** Gracious Home, New York, NY, (212) 231-7800. **magazine caddies and desk accessories:** Hold Everything, (888) 922-4117.

Chapter Five
Kitchens
PAGES 108-111 **for detailed information visit www.oprah.com** (search: jerry o'connell).
PAGES 112-115 **for detailed information visit www.oprah.com** (search: kirstie alley).

Chapter Six
Bedrooms
PAGES 124-127 **for detailed information visit www.oprah.com** (search: decorating disasters bedroom)
PAGES 124, 126 **lamps:** Crate & Barrel, (800) 967-6696.
PAGE 129 (top right) **headboard slipcover:** Pottery Barn, (888) 779-5176. **pillow shams, sheets, coverlet, blanket, throw:** Gracious Home, New York, NY, (212) 231-7800. **pillows with chain embroidery:** Linens-N-Things, (866) 568-7378. (bottom right) **throw, pillows, linens:** Linens-N-Things, (866) 568-7378.
PAGES 130-133 **for detailed information visit www.oprah.com** (search: ellin lavar).
PAGE 134 (top right) **headboard slipcover:** Pottery Barn, (888) 779-5176. **taupe pillow cases:** Crate & Barrel, (800) 967-6696. **light blue pillow cases, coverlet, throw on bench:** Gracious Home, New York, NY, (212) 231-7800. **silk boudoir pillow:** Portico, www.portico home. com. **ceramic bird:** Bedford & Company, New York, NY, (212) 772-7000. **basket tote:** Beads of Paradise, New York, NY, (212) 620-0642.
PAGES 136-137 **for detailed information visit www.oprah.com** (search: jerry o'connell).
PAGE 140 **headboard slipcover:** Pottery Barn, (888) 779-5176. **pillow shams, sheets, coverlet, blanket, throw:** Gracious Home, New York, NY, (212) 231-7800. **pillows with chain embroidery:** Linens-N-Things, (866) 568-7378.

Chapter Seven
Bathrooms
PAGE 144 **towels and basket:** Linens-N-Things, (866) 568-7378.
PAGES 146-147 **for detailed information visit www.oprah.com** (search: paige davis).
PAGES 150-151 **for detailed information visit www.oprah.com** (search: jerry o'connell).
PAGE 148 **sponge:** Gracious Home, New York, NY, (212) 231-7800.
PAGE 149 **stool:** Hold Everything, (888) 922-4117. **towels:** Gracious Home, New York, NY, (212) 231-7800.

Chapter Eight
Organizing
PAGES 160-161 **for detailed information visit www.oprah.com** (search: ellin lavar).
PAGE 162 **for detailed information visit www.oprah.com** (search: jenny lumet).
PAGE 163 **for detailed information visit www.oprah. com** (search: let the sun shine in).
PAGE 181 **for detailed information visit www.oprah.com** (search: oprah's office).

"your home should be a beautiful reflection of who you are and what you love"

photography credits

Fernando Bengoechea
8 (third from left), 30, 48, 50 (bottom),
51, 52, 53 (bottom), 56, 66, 68 (bottom),
69, 70, 71 (top), 73 (top left and bottom left),
104, 129 (top right), 130, 132 (bottom),
133, 154, 161, 162, 163.

John Bessler
3, 6 (top), 8 (second and fourth from left),
9 (first, second, and third from left), 10, 25
(top left, middle right, bottom left and bottom
center), 28, 34, 36-39, 40-45, 47(top center and
right, bottom left, center, right), 58, 64 (top right
and bottom left), 73 (top right), 74-78, 80-82,
86, 88-93, 94 (top left and bottom left), 96-102,
116-118, 122, 124, 126-127, 129 (top right
and bottom right), 134-135, 138, 140, 144,
147-149, 152, 166, 173 (top right).

Jonn Coolidge
50 (top), 53 (top).

François Dischinger
6 (bottom), 8 (first from left), 9 (fourth from left),
14, 16, 18-20, 23, 25 (top center and right,
middle left, bottom right), 27, 32, 47 (top left,
middle left, and middle right), 55, 60, 62, 64 (top
left), 84, 106, 120, 129 (top left), 142, 156, 158,
165, 168, 171, 172, 173 (bottom left), 176.

Andrew Eccles
1.

Pathway Creative
5.

Tim Street-Porter
7, 94 (top right), 108, 110-112, 114-115,
137, 151.

© 2003 Harpo Productions, Inc. All Rights Reserved. Photographer: George Burns

To the people who rule my world,
I thank you for believing in me from the very start

My love, respect, and admiration to

Oprah Winfrey, for waving the magic wand so gracefully, for raising my expectations of myself, and for making my dreams come true. **Ellen Rakieten,** for showing me a more beautiful world with her friendship, honesty, daily laughter, and for seeing me as I aspire to be. **Peter Kupferberg,** for being the older brother I never had, and the best one could hope for. **Kristin Giese,** for the thought behind it all, and for always leading with her heart. **Adam Glassman,** for being the final 10 percent, in every way. The **Bengoechea Family,** I will always be with you. **Barri Leiner,** for sharing her journey and joining me on mine. **Brooke and Scott Sandler,** for their friendship and for providing the Florida getaway. **Scott Seviour,** for sticking around all these years. **Lauren Buxbaum, Sasha Karp, Phoebe Craig, Annie Wasserman,** and **Allison Wilcox,** for bringing their creativity with them every day. **The fine women of Minnetonka,** who watch every show. **Jenna Kostelnik,** for raising her voice from the start. **Lisa Morin,** for her impeccable guidance. **Sheri Salata,** for lighting a candle and helping me to. **Lisa Erspamer,** for bringing me home. **Lisa Halliday,** for telling it like it is. **Harriet Seitler,** for telling it how it is. The whole **Harpo crew,** which has made this possible. The **O Magazine team,** for the incredible opportunity. **Nick and Zack Kupferberg** and **Charlie and Bill Coyle,** I hope you always jump as high as you can. **Emma Jayne** and **Quinn Conrad** for moving back into the picture. **John Smallwood,** for the incredible transformation. **Ruba Abu Nimah,** who is simply wonderful. **Taran Chernin** and the whole gang in Clifton, who help me bring it all home. **Dr. Sergio Narvaez,** for caving in for a while. **François Dischinger,** for his unquestionable eye. **Jan Miller and Michael Broussard,** for starting at square one. **Bob Miller,** for surviving more than just a dinner. **Will Schwalbe** and **Mary Ellen O'Neill,** for making the tough calls beautifully. **Rich Heller,** for being the voice of reason. **Anne Coyle,** for her great taste. **Sheila Starr,** for making me feel at home, and to the teams at **Hyperion** and **Smallwood & Stewart** for making it really rule.

And special thanks to my family

My mother, **Nancy Golden,** for the wisdom that enabled me to know myself. My father, **Michael Berkus,** for always going *Overboard*. **Dr. Marshall Golden,** for helping to turn it all around. **Sher Berkus,** for unlocking the mysteries buried in the garage. **Jesse Golden,** for surviving the penny loafer and becoming a man to admire. **Marni Golden,** for always winning the Thanksgiving Contest. **Steven Berkus,** for finally channeling his energy and for his generosity. **Dan Berkus,** for surviving the Yorba Linda pool incident. **Bob and Kelly Berkus,** love you two. **Doris and Mervin Levin,** for the Florida fan base. **Carl and Beatrice Berkus,** for making being a kid all it is supposed to be. **Lorraine and Sam Golden,** for their love and adventures. **Dr. Vicky Berkus,** for keeping us all together.